Good Housekeeping Cookery Club

DESSERTS

Linda Fraser

TED SMART

A TED SMART Publication 1995

1 3 5 7 9 10 8 6 4 2

Text and Photography © Ebury Press 1994

First published in the United Kingdom in 1994 by
Ebury Press Random House, 20 Vauxhall Bridge Road, London SW1V 2SA

Random House Australia (Pty) Limited
20 Alfred Street, Milsons Point, Sydney,
New South Wales 2061, Australia

Random House New Zealand Limited
18 Poland Road, Glenfield,
Auckland 10, New Zealand

Random House South Africa (Pty) Limited
PO Box 337, Bergvlei, South Africa

Random House UK Limited Reg. No. 954009

A CIP catalogue record for this book is available from the British Library.

Managing Editor: JANET ILLSLEY
Design: SARA KIDD
Special Photography: GUS FILGATE
Food Stylist: MAXINE CLARK
Photographic Stylist: SUZI GITTINGS
Techniques Photography: KARL ADAMSON
Food Techniques Stylist: ANNIE NICHOLS
Recipe Testing: EMMA-LEE GOW

ISBN 0 09 180546 5

Typeset in Gill Sans by Textype Typesetters, Cambridge
Colour Separations by Magnacraft, London
Printed and bound in Italy by New Interlitho Italia S.p.a., Milan

CONTENTS

COOKERY NOTES

- Both metric and imperial measures are given for the recipes. Follow either metric or imperial throughout as they are not interchangeable.
- All spoon measures are level unless otherwise stated. Sets of measuring spoons are available in metric and imperial for accurate measurement of small quantities.
- Ovens should be preheated to the specified temperature. Grills should also be preheated. The cooking times given in the recipes assume that this has been done.
- Cooking times can vary significantly between individual ovens. Start checking to see whether the dish is cooked towards the end of the suggested cooking time.
- Where a stage is specified in brackets under freezing instructions, the dish should be frozen at the end of that stage.
- Size 2 eggs should be used except where otherwise specified.

INTRODUCTION

Desserts are enjoying a renaissance and, for everyone who is partial to something sweet at the end of a meal, it's a welcome return. The revival is due partly, I'm sure, to the wealth of new exotic fruits and interesting ingredients to be found in delicatessens, good food halls and supermarkets.

Many British puddings considered to be out-dated have been given a new look and a new lease of life – Bread and Butter Pudding (page 20), made with croissants and a creamy vanilla-scented custard is quite simply scrumptious, and rice pudding (page 22), lightened with egg whites and baked with caramel in individual pots could be served at the smartest of dinner parties.

The secret of the perfect dessert, first and foremost, is to make the right choice – don't choose the recipe without considering the rest of the meal. The dessert must complement the other courses, in terms of flavour, texture, weight and colour – to ensure variety. If the main course or starter includes pastry, for instance, avoid this for the dessert. When you are serving a rich, or heavy main course, balance it with a light or fruity pudding; if the proceeding courses are light, then you can be as indulgent as you like.

Your choice will also depend on the time available for advance preparation. Frozen desserts, sorbets and ice creams can be made weeks in advance, if you like, and many other recipes can be frozen ready to defrost when you need them. You'll find some surprises – the Hot Mango Soufflés (page 26) can be prepared and frozen ready to bake while you eat the main course! Most of the cakes, gâteaux and puddings can be prepared either partly or completely in advance and others, such as the Crème Fraîche Crèmets (page 34) and Summer Pudding (page 52), really must be made the day before you eat them – ideal choices if you are likely to be short of time on the day.

The time of year may affect your choice too. Although the seasons are becoming blurred as fruits are now flown in all-year round from different parts of the world, out-of-season fruits such as strawberries and peaches are often quite tasteless in winter – and expensive too. Choose a dessert that suits the season, when the ingredients are at their most abundant and flavoursome – opt for apples, pears and blackberries in autumn; citrus fruits in winter; melons and rhubarb in the spring and early summer and, of course, summer fruits in summer!

All of the recipes have preparation and cooking times so you know exactly how much time you need. Step-by-step photographs illustrate many of the processes and tricky techniques, and there are plenty of special tips to help you too. You also have the added reassurance that all recipes have been double tested in the Good Housekeeping kitchens.

Some of the recipes have several parts and at first glance may seem complicated or time-consuming to make. For impromptu occasions, or whenever you are short of time, simplify the dishes by serving ready-made biscuits, or a good shop-bought ice cream or sorbet, instead of making your own. And if you haven't the time – or the ingredients to hand – to make a sauce you can simply add a dollop of thick yogurt, cream or crème fraîche. Thankfully, we don't reserve desserts solely for special occasions; you will find recipes here that are simple to make, use light, healthy ingredients and are ideal for rounding off any meal.

Whenever you serve a dessert consider the finishing touches. There's no need for elaborate decorations, even for special occasions. More often than not, a simple presentation has more impact – just a glance at the fabulous photographs will show how a dusting of icing sugar or cocoa, or a scattering of fresh fruit or chocolate curls can give the most spectacular effect.

PASTRY-MAKING

Fruit-filled flans and pies are an ideal way of making the most of fruits in season. Pâte Sucrée is the classic French rich short pastry used for sweet flans; it is thin and crisp, yet melting in texture. Flan pastry is an enriched sweetened shortcrust pastry, which is quick and easy to make. Both of these pastries benefit from being left to rest in the refrigerator for at least 30 minutes before rolling out. Both pastries are also suitable for freezing.

PÂTE SUCRÉE
100 g (4 oz) plain flour
pinch of salt
50 g (2 oz) butter (at room
temperature)
2 egg yolks
50 g (2 oz) caster sugar

1. Sift the flour and salt onto a work surface. Make a well in the centre and add the butter, egg yolks and sugar.

2. Using the fingertips of one hand, work the sugar, butter and egg yolks together until well blended.

3. Gradually work in all the flour to bind the mixture together.

4. Knead lightly until smooth, then wrap the pastry in foil or cling film and leave to rest in the refrigerator or a cool place for at least 30 minutes.

FLAN PASTRY
100 g (4 oz) plain flour
pinch of salt
75 g (3 oz) butter or margarine,
  chilled and diced
5 ml (1 tsp) caster sugar
1 egg, beaten

1. Sift the flour and salt into a bowl. Lightly rub in the fat, using your fingertips, until the mixture resembles fine breadcrumbs.

2. Sprinkle in the sugar and stir in lightly.

3. Add the egg, stirring with a round-bladed knife until the ingredients begin to stick together in large lumps.

4. With one hand, collect the mixture together and knead lightly for a few seconds to give a firm, smooth dough. Wrap the pastry in foil or cling film and leave to rest in the refrigerator or a cool place for at least 30 minutes.

PUFF PASTRY

The richest of all the pastries, puff requires patience, practice and very light handling. Whenever possible it should be made the day before use. It is not practical to make in a quantity with less than 450 g (1 lb) flour weight. Ready-made puff pastry is widely available, both fresh and frozen. This quantity is equivalent to two 375 g (13 oz) packets of ready-made puff.

450 g (1 lb) strong plain flour
pinch of salt
450 g (1 lb) butter or margarine,
 chilled
15 ml (1 tbsp) lemon juice

1. Mix the flour and salt together in a bowl. Slice off 50 g (2 oz) of the butter and cut into dice. Flatten the remaining butter with a rolling pin to a slab 2 cm (¾ inch) thick.

2. Rub the diced butter into the flour. Using a round-bladed knife, stir in the lemon juice and about 300 ml (½ pint) chilled water or sufficient to make a soft dough.

3. Quickly knead the dough until smooth and shape into a round. Cut through half the depth in the shape of a cross. Open out to form a star.

4. Roll out, keeping the centre four times as thick as the flaps. Place the slab of butter in the centre.

ROLLING OUT PASTRY

5. Fold the flaps envelope-style gently with a rolling pin. Roll out to a 40 x 20 cm (16 x 8 inch) rectangle.

6. Fold the bottom third up and the top third down, keeping the edges straight. Seal the edges. Wrap in cling film and leave to rest in the refrigerator for 30 minutes.

7. Put the pastry on a lightly floured surface with the folded edges to the sides, then repeat the rolling, folding and resting sequence five times.

Sprinkle a little flour on the work surface and the rolling pin (not the pastry) and roll out the dough evenly in one direction only.

LINING A FLAN CASE

Loose-based metal flan tins are ideal because they transfer heat rapidly and pastry tends to cook better in these than in china dishes. The removable base makes it easier to transfer the baked flan to a serving plate. Alternatively use a flan ring placed on a baking sheet, a sandwich tin or a fluted china flan dish.

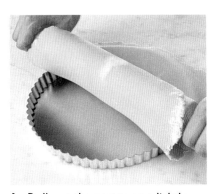

1. Roll out the pastry on a lightly floured surface until it is about 5 cm (2 inches) larger than the flan tin all round. Use the rolling pin to help you carefully lift the pastry over the flan tin.

2. Lift the edges of the pastry so that it falls down into the tin, then gently press the pastry against the edges of the flan tin so that there are no gaps between the pastry and the tin.

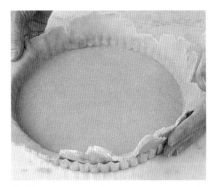

3. Turn any surplus pastry outwards over the rim of the flan tin and trim the pastry edges with a sharp knife to neaten. Alternatively, you can roll the rolling pin over the top of the tin to cut off excess pastry.

BAKING BLIND

If a recipe instructs you to bake blind, it means that you should bake the pastry case (or cases) without any filling. The pastry may be partially cooked before adding the filling, or it may be completely cooked if the filling doesn't require further cooking.

Fully baked pastry cases will keep for several days in an airtight tin or they may be frozen.

1. Line the flan tin or dish with pastry. If you have time, chill the pastry case in the refrigerator for 20-30 minutes to rest the pastry and help reduce shrinkage during cooking. Prick the pastry base with a fork, then line with a piece of greaseproof paper or foil which is larger than the pastry case.

2. Fill with ceramic baking beans or dried pulses. Tartlet cases don't need lining; it should be sufficient to prick these with a fork.

3. For partially baked cases, bake at 200°F (400°F) mark 6 for 10-15 minutes until the case looks 'set'. Carefully remove the paper or foil and the beans and bake for a further 5 minutes until the base is firm to the touch and lightly coloured. Pastry cases which need complete baking should be returned to the oven for about 15 minutes until firm and golden brown.

COVERING A PIE DISH

1. Using the inverted pie dish as a guide, roll out the pastry until 5 cm (2 inches) larger than the pie dish. Cut a 2.5 cm (1 inch) strip from the outside of the pastry. Place on the moistened rim of the pie dish and brush with water.

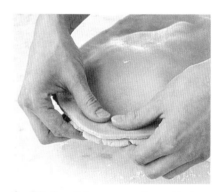

2. Fill the dish generously, so that the surface of the filling is slightly rounded; use a pie funnel if insufficient filling is available. Use the rolling pin to help lift the pastry lid into position. Press the edges together to seal.

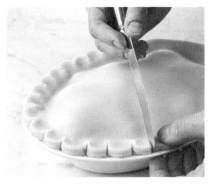

3. Using a sharp knife held at a slight angle away from the dish, trim off excess pastry. Knock up the edges and finish as desired (see right).

FINISHING TOUCHES

Decorative edges and applied pastry shapes look attractive. Remember to glaze the decoration as well as the pie or flan.

FLUTED OR SCALLOPED EDGE: Press your thumb on the rim of the pastry and at the same time gently draw back the floured blade of a round-bladed knife about 1 cm (½ inch) towards the centre. Repeat around the pie at 2.5 cm (1 inch) intervals.

FORKED EDGE: Simply press all around the edges of the pie with the back of a floured fork.

LEAVES: Cut 2.5 cm (1 inch) strips from pastry trimmings, then cut these diagonally into diamonds. Use the back of a knife to mark veins.

KNOCK UP: This seals the edges and prevents the filling leaking out. Press your index finger along the rim and holding a knife horizontally, tap the edge of the pastry sharply with the blunt edge of the knife to give a 'flaky' appearance.

CRIMPED EDGE: Push your forefinger into the rim of the pastry and using the thumb and forefinger of the other hand gently pinch the pastry that is pushed up by this action. Continue evenly around the edge of the pie.

OTHER DECORATIONS: Although leaves are the traditional decoration for pies, different shapes can be cut freehand or using cutters. Holly leaves are ideal for festive pies.

TARTE TATIN

This classic French pudding is cooked upside down. Apples are cooked first in a buttery caramel, then covered with a layer of pastry. After baking the tart is turned over so the fruit layer is on top and the buttery, caramel juices ooze into the crisp puffy crust. Serve it warm with a scoop of vanilla ice cream.

SERVES 6

225 g (8 oz) ready-made puff
    pastry (see note)
FILLING
75 g (3 oz) caster sugar
4-5 eating apples
50 g (2 oz) unsalted butter,
    in pieces

PREPARATION TIME
25 minutes
COOKING TIME
25-30 minutes
FREEZING
Not suitable

310 CALS PER SERVING

1. First make the filling. Put the sugar in a saucepan with 45 ml (3 tbsp) water. Dissolve over a low heat, stirring occasionally, then increase the heat and without stirring, cook the syrup to a rich brown caramel. Carefully pour into a shallow heavy-based 20 cm (8 inch) cake tin or ovenproof frying pan and swirl round to coat the base of the tin evenly with caramel.

2. Preheat the oven to 220°C (425°F) Mark 7. Cut the apples in half, then peel them and scoop out the cores, using a teaspoon.

3. Dot the caramel with half of the butter. Arrange the apple halves curved side down on top, packing them as tightly as possible. Fill any gaps with smaller wedges of apple. Dot the remaining butter on top. Place the tin or pan over a medium heat and cook for about 5 minutes to par-cook and lightly brown the apples. Watch carefully to ensure the apples do not burn.

4. Roll out the puff pastry on a lightly floured surface to a round, slightly larger than the diameter of the tin or pan. Prick all over with a fork. Carefully lift the pastry round and place on top of the apples. Pat down gently, tucking the edges of the pastry down the side of the tin. Bake in the oven for 20-25 minutes until the pastry is well risen, crisp and golden brown.

5. Allow to cool for 10 minutes. To remove from the tin, cover with a large serving plate, carefully tip out any cooking juices into a bowl, then turn the tin and plate over. Give the base of the tin a few sharp taps with a rolling pin, then carefully lift off. Drizzle over the buttery juices and serve at once, cut into wedges, with a dollop or two of vanilla ice cream.

NOTE: If you have time, make your own puff pastry according to the step-by-step recipe on page 6. You will need approximately one third of the quantity.

VARIATION

Replace the apple with 3 large ripe, richly scented mangoes. Peel, then cut the flesh from the stone into large wedges. If the mangoes are very ripe and soft, omit the cooking on the hob.

TECHNIQUE

Lift the pastry round over the apples, making sure they are completely covered.

RASPBERRY AND VANILLA CUSTARD TART

In this summer tart, flavourful raspberries sit atop a creamy vanilla custard, with a liberal dusting of vanilla sugar. Take care to avoid overcooking the custard filling – it should still wobble slightly in the centre when it is done, so that the end result is softly set with a smooth velvet texture. Serve with crème fraîche or single cream.

SERVES 6

FLAN PASTRY
175 g (6 oz) plain flour
125 g (4 oz) butter, in pieces
25 g (1 oz) vanilla sugar (see note)
5 ml (1 tsp) finely grated orange rind
1 egg yolk
VANILLA CUSTARD
2 eggs
2 egg yolks
40 g (1½ oz) caster sugar
½ vanilla pod
450 ml (¾ pint) single cream
TO FINISH
175 g (6 oz) raspberries
vanilla sugar, for dusting

PREPARATION TIME
40 minutes, plus cooling
COOKING TIME
About 1 hour
FREEZING
Suitable: Pastry case only

510 CALS PER SERVING

1. To make the pastry, sift the flour into a bowl. Rub in the butter, using your fingertips. Add the vanilla sugar and grated orange rind, then using a round-bladed knife, mix in the egg yolk, together with 10-15 ml (2-3 tsp) cold water, as necessary to form a stiff dough.

2. Knead the pastry dough briefly until smooth. Wrap in cling film and chill in the refrigerator for about 20 minutes.

3. Preheat the oven to 200°C (400°F) Mark 6. Butter a 4 cm (1½ inch) deep, 20 cm (8 inch) loose-based fluted flan tin.

4. Roll out the dough on a lightly floured surface and use to line the prepared flan tin. Chill again for 20 minutes. Line the pastry case with greaseproof paper or foil and baking beans and bake 'blind' for 15 minutes. Remove the baking beans and paper or foil and return to the oven for 5-10 minutes to cook the base.

5. To make the custard filling, put the whole eggs, egg yolks and sugar in a bowl and beat well. Split the vanilla pod, scrape out the seeds and place both in a small pan with the cream. Cook over a very low heat until the cream is well flavoured and almost boiling. Pour on to the egg mixture, whisking constantly, then strain into the pastry case.

6. Lower the oven temperature to 150°C (300°F) Mark 2. Place the tart in the oven and bake for 45 minutes or until the centre is lightly set. Remove from the oven and leave until cold.

7. Carefully remove the flan from the tin. To finish, arrange the raspberries on top of the vanilla custard. Dust liberally with vanilla sugar to serve.

NOTE: Vanilla sugar can be bought in small jars and sachets, but make sure you avoid buying inferior, synthetic substitutes. To flavour your own sugar with the subtle scent of true vanilla, simply store one or two vanilla pods in an airtight jar of caster sugar. After a couple of days the sugar will be ready. The sugar level can be topped up as you use it.

TECHNIQUE

Strain the vanilla custard through a fine-meshed sieve into the pastry case.

WALNUT AND FIG TART

This is a gorgeous, dark treacly tart with a moist, sticky layer of figs encased in a crumbly pastry case – with walnuts adding a nutty crunch. To offset the sweet taste of the tart, serve, still warm, with crème fraîche. This lovely, almost lemony, soured cream from France is becoming increasingly available from large supermarkets. Alternatively top with a dollop or two of whipped cream.

SERVES 8

PASTRY
175 g (6 oz) plain flour
pinch of salt
125 g (4 oz) unsalted butter
   (at room temperature), in
   pieces
2 egg yolks
FILLING
150 g (5 oz) ready-to-eat
   dried figs
100 g (3½ oz) fresh white
   breadcrumbs
90 ml (6 tbsp) molasses or
   dark treacle
135 ml (9 tbsp) golden syrup
30 ml (2 tbsp) lemon juice
125 g (4 oz) shelled walnuts

PREPARATION TIME
50 minutes, plus cooling
COOKING TIME
40-50 minutes
FREEZING
Suitable: Stage 5. Thaw for 3-4
hours, then bake as above.

470 CALS PER SERVING

1. To make the pastry, sift the flour and salt into a mound on a work surface. Make a well in the centre. Add the butter, egg yolks and 15 ml (1 tbsp) cold water to the well. Using the fingertips of one hand, work the ingredients together to form a soft dough, adding a little extra water, if necessary. Knead very lightly until smooth, then form into a flat round. Wrap in a polythene bag and chill for 30 minutes.

2. Preheat the oven to 200°C (400°F) Mark 6. Roll out the dough on a lightly floured surface and use to line a 23 cm (9 inch) loose-based flan tin. Prick the base with a fork and chill for 10 minutes.

3. To make the filling, trim the stems from the figs, then cut into small chunks. Scatter evenly over the base of the tart.

4. Put the breadcrumbs, molasses or treacle, golden syrup and lemon juice in a food processor or blender and process briefly until just combined. Add 75 g (3 oz) of the walnuts and whizz for a few seconds until they are cut into rough chunks. (Alternatively chop the walnuts by hand, then thoroughly mix with the rest of the filling ingredients in a large bowl.)

5. Line the pastry case with greaseproof paper or foil and baking beans. Bake in the oven for 15 minutes, then remove the paper or foil and beans and bake for 5-10 minutes longer to cook the base.

Spoon the filling into the pastry case and spread evenly over the figs.

6. Arrange the reserved walnuts on top, press them down gently and bake in the oven for 20-25 minutes until the filling is just firm. Remove the tart from the oven and leave to cool to room temperature before serving, with crème fraîche.

NOTE: To weigh molasses and golden syrup accurately, warm the tins by standing them in a pan of hot water before measuring out level spoonfuls.

VARIATION

Replace the walnuts in the filling with pecan nuts. When making the pastry, add 50 ml (2 tbsp) each cocoa powder and caster sugar to the flour and increase the water to 30 ml (2 tbsp).

TECHNIQUE

Spoon the treacle filling over the dried figs in the flan case and spread evenly.

PEACH CROUSTADE

For this hot summer pie, fresh peaches are cooked in a buttery caramel sauce, then encased in delicate filo pastry. The pie is dusted liberally with caster sugar and baked until the crumbled pastry top is dark golden brown, very crisp and caramelised. The recipe is based on a traditional French pie.

SERVES 6

6 large, ripe peaches

100 g (3½ oz) unsalted butter

45 ml (3 tbsp) armagnac (or other brandy)

175 g (6 oz) caster sugar

1 packet filo pastry, about 225 g (8 oz) (see note)

PREPARATION TIME
40 minutes
COOKING TIME
35-40 minutes
FREEZING
Not suitable

385 CALS PER SERVING

1. Immerse the peaches in a large bowl of boiling water for 30 seconds, then lift out with a slotted spoon and slip off the skins. Halve and stone the peaches, then cut into thick slices.

2. Melt half of the butter in a frying pan, add the peach slices and sprinkle with the armagnac and half of the sugar. Cook over a medium heat for 3-5 minutes until just tender, then leave to cool.

3. Preheat the oven to 200°C (400°F) Mark 6. Melt the remaining butter in a small pan and use a little to butter a 23 cm (9 inch) flan tin. Sprinkle 15 ml (1 tbsp) of the remaining sugar over the base of the tin.

4. Lay one sheet of filo pastry in the flan tin, allowing the corners to overlap the edge of the tin. Brush with a little of the butter, then repeat with two more sheets of filo.

5. Spoon the peaches and buttery juices into the flan tin. Flip the corners of the filo into the flan tin, then, one at a time, brush the remaining sheets of filo with butter. Crumple them and arrange on top of the peaches, covering the fruit completely. Tuck in the edges neatly down the side of the tin.

6. Sprinkle the remaining butter and sugar over the top, then bake for 20 minutes. Reduce the oven temperature

to 180°C (350°F) Mark 4 and bake for a further 15-20 minutes until the pastry is crisp and golden and the sugar has caramelised. Serve warm with cream.

NOTE: Filo pastry sheets come in a variety of shapes and sizes, but the shape isn't too crucial in this recipe. Make sure though that, when you arrange the first three sheets, the corners are staggered so the tin is lined evenly.

TECHNIQUE

Immersing the peaches in boiling water loosens the skins, so they can then be peeled away quite easily.

BRAMBLE AND APPLE CRUMBLE WITH LEMON ICE

It's fashionable to serve hot puddings with ice cream – and here, the combination of hot, autumn fruits and crisp crumble with lemon yogurt ice is scrummy! The ice cream takes 3-4 hours to freeze, so either make it to serve as soon as it is firm; or freeze ahead and allow to soften in the refrigerator for 20 minutes before serving.

SERVES 6

CRUMBLE TOPPING

50 g (2 oz) plain flour

25 g (1 oz) plain wholemeal
   flour

75 g (3 oz) muscovado sugar

50 g (2 oz) ground almonds

50 g (2 oz) unsalted butter

FILLING

575 g (1¼ lb) eating apples

50 g (2 oz) unsalted butter

50 g (2 oz) caster sugar

30 ml (2 tbsp) Calvados
   (apple brandy) (optional)

225 g (8 oz) blackberries

LEMON YOGURT ICE

3-4 large lemons

2 eggs

2 egg yolks

200 g (7 oz) caster sugar

75 g (3 oz) unsalted butter,
   in pieces

500 g (1 lb 2 oz) Greek
   strained yogurt

PREPARATION TIME
45 minutes, plus freezing
COOKING TIME
25 minutes
FREEZING
Suitable: Ice cream and crumble
topping only (stage 4).

730 CALS PER SERVING

1. First make the lemon yogurt ice. Finely grate the rind from the lemons and place in a heatproof bowl. Beat together the whole eggs and egg yolks, then strain on to the lemon rind. Add the sugar and butter. Squeeze the juice from the lemons and add 175 ml (6 fl oz) to the bowl.

2. Place bowl over a pan of simmering water and stir for about 20 minutes, until the sugar dissolves and the mixture thickens. Remove the bowl from the pan and leave to cool, stirring occasionally.

3. When the lemon mixture is cold, fold it into the yogurt until evenly blended, then pour into a freezerproof container. Freeze for about 3-4 hours until firm.

4. To make the crumble topping, sift the flours into a bowl, then tip in any bran from the sieve. Stir in the sugar and ground almonds, then work in the butter using your fingertips to make a very crumbly mixture. Set aside.

5. Preheat the oven to 190°C (375°F) Mark 5. Butter a 1.7 litre (3 pint) oven-proof dish.

6. Quarter the apples, then peel, core and cut into 2.5 cm (1 inch) chunks. Melt the butter in a large frying pan. Add the apples, with the sugar, and cook, stirring, over a high heat for 3-5 minutes until golden brown and tender.

7. In a small pan, warm the Calvados, if using. Ignite it and pour over the apples, then spread in the ovenproof dish. Scatter the blackberries on top. Spoon over the crumble topping and bake in the oven for 25 minutes until the topping is golden brown. Serve warm, with a spoonful or two of the ice cream.

VARIATION

Replace the brambles with 225 g (8 oz) mixed summer fruits, such as red and blackcurrants, raspberries and stoned cherries. In the winter, use frozen fruits.

TECHNIQUE

To make the crumble topping, lightly rub the butter into the flour, sugar and ground almond mixture – using your fingertips.

BREAD AND BUTTER PUDDING

Traditional puds, like this one, are enjoying something of a renaissance. Here, light and flaky croissants replace the usual bread. The baking dish is set in a bain-marie, so the custard cooks to a quite blissful consistency – only just softly set and wonderfully creamy. Soak the sultanas in a little brandy to plump them up, if you like. Serve the pudding just warm, with double or clotted cream.

SERVES 6

4 large croissants (see note)
75 g (3 oz) unsalted butter
    (at room temperature)
50 g (2 oz) sultanas
CUSTARD
300 ml (½ pint) milk
    (at room temperature)
300 ml (½ pint) double
    cream (at room
    temperature)
1 vanilla pod, split
6 egg yolks
125 g (4 oz) caster sugar
TO FINISH
15 ml (1 tbsp) icing sugar,
    for dusting

PREPARATION TIME
15 minutes
COOKING TIME
45-50 minutes
FREEZING
Suitable: Before baking

645 CALS PER SERVING

1. Preheat the oven to 180°C (350°F) Mark 4. Butter a 1.7 litre (3 pint) shallow baking dish.

2. Slice the croissants thickly, then spread with the butter. Arrange the croissant slices, butter-side up and over-lapping, in the prepared dish, scattering in the sultanas as you do so.

3. To make the custard, pour the milk and cream into a saucepan. Add the vanilla pod and place over a very low heat for about 5 minutes until the mixture is almost boiling and well flavoured with vanilla.

4. Meanwhile, in a large bowl, whisk together the egg yolks and caster sugar until light and foamy. Strain the flavoured milk on to the egg mixture, whisking all the time.

5. Pour the egg mixture evenly over the croissants. Place the dish in a bain-marie or large roasting tin and pour in enough boiling water to come half-way up the sides of the dish. Bake in the oven for 45-50 minutes until the custard is softly set and the top is crisp and golden.

6. Remove from the oven and leave the pudding in the bain-marie until just

warm. Sprinkle with the icing sugar and serve with cream.

NOTE: The croissants are better used when slightly stale. Leave them in a cool place for a day or two, to dry and firm up before slicing.

VARIATION

Replace the croissants with 4-6 individual brioche (depending on size) and substitute roughly chopped, ready-to-eat dried apricots for the sultanas. When preparing the custard, flavour with the pared rind of 1 orange instead of the vanilla pod.

TECHNIQUE

Cut the croissants into thick slices, then spread with butter.

CARAMEL RICE PUDDINGS WITH EXOTIC FRUITS

This feather-light version of rice pudding is flavoured with a hint of lemon and vanilla, then baked in caramel-coated individual dishes, before being turned out to serve with tangy, exotic fruits. Take care when you are preparing the caramel – and don't let it become too dark or it will taste bitter.

RICE PUDDINGS
25 g (1 oz) unsalted butter
500 ml (16 fl oz) milk
½ vanilla pod
finely pared rind of 1 lemon
125 g (4 oz) short-grain
     pudding rice
175 g (6 oz) sugar
2 eggs, separated
EXOTIC FRUITS
½ pineapple
2 papayas
15 ml (1 tbsp) caster sugar
juice and grated rind of
     1 large orange

PREPARATION TIME
30 minutes
COOKING TIME
1-1¼ hours
FREEZING
Not suitable

355 CALS PER SERVING

1. First make the rice puddings. Preheat the oven to 150°C (300°F) Mark 2. Use the butter to grease six 150 ml (¼ pint) individual pudding basins or ramekins.

2. Pour the milk into a saucepan. Split the vanilla pod in half lengthways and add to the pan with the lemon rind. Bring slowly to the boil, then stir in the rice and cover the pan. Cook over a very low heat, so the milk is just simmering, for 20-25 minutes until the rice is tender and creamy. Remove the pan from the heat, stir in half of the sugar and leave to cool.

3. Put the remaining sugar in a heavy-based pan with 90 ml (6 tbsp) water. Dissolve over a low heat, stirring occasionally, then increase the heat and cook, without stirring, to a rich caramel colour. Immediately pour into the prepared moulds, tilting them to coat the base and sides. Set aside.

4. Remove the lemon rind and vanilla pod from the rice. Scrape the seeds out from inside the vanilla pod and stir them into the rice with the egg yolks. Whisk the egg whites in a large bowl until holding soft peaks, then fold into the rice. Divide the rice evenly between the pudding basins or ramekins. Place in a roasting tin and pour in boiling water to a

depth of 2.5 cm (1 inch). Bake in the oven for 45-50 minutes, or until slightly risen and just firm.

5. Meanwhile, cut the pineapple into 1 cm (½ inch) slices, then remove the skin and 'eyes' using a sharp knife. Stamp out the core using a small round cutter, then cut into chunks. Halve the papayas and scoop out the seeds, then peel and cut into chunks. Place the fruits in a bowl with the sugar, orange rind and juice; toss lightly to mix.

6. When the rice puddings are ready, run a sharp knife around each one, then gently turn out on to individual serving plates. Spoon some of the fruit and juices around each pudding and serve at once.

TECHNIQUE

Carefully pour the hot caramel into the greased individual moulds and tilt them to coat the base and sides.

CHOCOLATE BROWNIES WITH SPICED ORANGES

These gooey squares are often served at tea-time, but here they make a superb pudding – enriched with melting chunks of chocolate and served with a cool spiced orange compote. Use good quality Swiss or Belgian chocolate for optimum flavour. Don't overcook the cake – after baking it should still be soft and very moist in the middle with a thin crisp crust on top.

SERVES 8

125 g (4 oz) skinned
   hazelnuts
125 g (4 oz) butter
175 g (6 oz) plain chocolate
175 g (6 oz) light muscovado
   sugar
2 eggs, beaten
few drops of vanilla essence
50 g (2 oz) plain flour
pinch of salt
5 ml (1 tsp) baking powder
SPICED ORANGES
125 g (4 oz) caster sugar
½ cinnamon stick
2 cloves
1 star anise
3 oranges
TO FINISH
15 ml (1 tbsp) icing sugar,
   for dusting

PREPARATION TIME
30 minutes, plus cooling
COOKING TIME
About 50 minutes
FREEZING
Suitable: Thaw at room
temperature; warm cake in oven
before serving.

465 CALS PER SERVING

1. Preheat the oven to 180°C (350°F) Mark 4. Grease and line an 18 cm (7 inch) square shallow baking tin, making sure that the paper extends about 5 cm (2 inches) above the rim of the tin. Spread out the hazelnuts on a baking sheet and bake in the oven for 15-20 minutes until browned. Leave to cool, then chop coarsely.

2. Melt the butter with 50 g (2 oz) of the chocolate in a heatproof bowl over a pan of hot water. Place the sugar, eggs and vanilla essence in a large bowl, then sift in the flour, salt and baking powder. Pour in the melted mixture and stir together, gently yet thoroughly, until well mixed.

3. Chop the remaining chocolate into rough chunks and stir into the brownie mixture, with the hazelnuts. Spoon the mixture into the prepared tin and spread evenly. Bake in the oven for 50 minutes or until the cake begins to shrink from the sides of the tin and the centre is springy to touch.

4. While the cake is cooking, prepare the spiced oranges. Place the sugar in a pan with 150 ml (¼ pint) water and dissolve over a low heat, stirring occasionally. Add the spices and bring the syrup

to the boil. Boil for 2 minutes, then remove from the heat and set aside.

5. Working on a large plate to catch the juices, remove the peel and all the white pith from the oranges, using a serrated knife. Cut the oranges into 5 mm (¼ inch) thick slices and place in a bowl. Pour on the syrup, together with any orange juice. Leave to cool.

6. Leave the cake to cool in the tin for 30 minutes until warm, then lift out by the paper. Carefully peel off the lining paper and transfer to a board. Cut into 16 squares and dust with a little icing sugar. Serve the chocolate brownies slightly warm, with the spiced oranges.

TECHNIQUE

Spoon the mixture into the lined baking tin and spread out evenly with the back of the spoon.

HOT MANGO SOUFFLÉS WITH PAPAYA SAUCE

These little fruit flavoured soufflés are turned out while hot onto a pool of slightly sharp, scented papaya sauce – and the crunchy almond layer in the base becomes a nutty, golden topping. The thought of tipping a hot soufflé out of its dish to serve should worry even the most confident cook, but this recipe works like a dream.

SERVES 6

50 g (2 oz) butter, melted

150 g (5 oz) caster sugar

25 g (1 oz) blanched
  almonds

2 ripe mangoes, each about
  350 g (12 oz)

20 ml (4 tsp) cornflour

30 ml (2 tbsp) orange juice

5 ml (1 tsp) finely grated
  orange rind

6 egg whites

PAPAYA SAUCE

2-3 papayas

30-45 ml (2-3 tbsp) caster
  sugar

10-15 ml (2-3 tsp) lemon
  juice

PREPARATION TIME
55 minutes
COOKING TIME
6-8 minutes
FREEZING
Suitable: Before baking; thaw
soufflés at room temperature
for 2 hours, then bake.

310 CALS PER SERVING

1. Brush 6 deep ramekins with the butter, evenly and generously, then dust with 40 g (1½ oz) of the sugar, tapping out any excess. Chop the almonds coarsely and divide between the ramekins.

2. Peel the mangoes and cut the flesh away from the stones. Purée the mango flesh in a food processor or blender until smooth.

3. Pour the mango purée into a small, heavy-based saucepan and cook over a low heat for 20 minutes, stirring frequently, until reduced to a thick paste.

4. Put the remaining 90 g (3½ oz) sugar in a small heavy-based pan, with 45 ml (3 tbsp) water and dissolve over a low heat, stirring occasionally. Boil rapidly for 2 minutes, then stir the syrup into the mango purée.

5. Blend the cornflour with the orange juice and stir into the mango purée, with the orange rind. Cook, stirring, over a medium heat until boiling and thickened. Remove from the heat and cover the surface with dampened greaseproof paper; set aside to cool.

6. Meanwhile, make the papaya sauce. Halve the papayas, scoop out the seeds, then peel. Purée the flesh in a food processor or blender. Add sugar and lemon juice to taste; set aside.

7. Preheat the oven to 220°C (425°F) Mark 7 and preheat a baking sheet. Whisk the egg whites in a large bowl until holding soft peaks, then whisk one third into the mango mixture. Carefully fold in the remaining egg whites.

8. Spoon the mixture into the ramekins – the dishes should be full. Place on the preheated baking sheet and bake just above the centre of the oven for 6-8 minutes until well risen and golden.

9. Meanwhile, spoon the papaya sauce on to individual plates. When the soufflés are ready, gently unmould them on to the sauce and serve at once.

TECHNIQUE

Lightly fold the whisked egg whites into the mango mixture, using a large spatula.

PASSION FRUIT SOUFFLÉS

This wonderfully intense passion fruit mousse is set in ragged, dark chocolate cups and served in a pool of passion fruit sauce. Peel off the foil while the soufflés are still firm, then allow them to return to room temperature before serving, so they become soft, fluffy and full of flavour.

SERVES 6

12 passion fruit
175 g (6 oz) caster sugar
3 eggs, separated
juice of ½ lemon
11 g (0.4 oz) sachet
    powdered gelatine
300 ml (½ pint) double
    cream
5-10 ml (1-2 tsp) arrowroot
juice of 1 large orange
CHOCOLATE CUPS
175 g (6 oz) plain chocolate,
    in pieces

PREPARATION TIME
1 hour 10 minutes, plus chilling
COOKING TIME
Nil
FREEZING
Suitable: Thaw overnight in the refrigerator, or for 2-3 hours at room temperature.

550 CALS PER SERVING

1. First make the chocolate cups. Melt the chocolate in a heatproof bowl over a pan of hot water. Cut six 23 cm (9 inch) rounds of foil and use to line six ramekins, crumpling the foil to fit – it will stand above the rims. Brush evenly with the melted chocolate, leaving the top edge ragged. Place in the refrigerator to set.

2. Halve the passion fruits and scoop out the pulp and seeds into a small pan. Add the sugar and 15 ml (1 tbsp) water and stir over a low heat until hot, but not boiling. Tip the mixture into a nylon sieve over a large heatproof bowl and, using a wooden spoon, push through as much pulp as possible. Reserve 15 ml (1 tbsp) of the seeds.

3. Set aside one third of the passion fruit pulp. Add the egg yolks to the remaining pulp and place the bowl over a pan of barely simmering water. Beat vigorously with an electric beater or balloon whisk for about 20 minutes until the mixture is light and thick. Remove the basin from the heat and set aside.

4. Place the lemon juice in a small heatproof bowl, sprinkle over the gelatine and leave to swell for a few minutes. Then stand the bowl in a pan of hot water and dissolve over a low heat. Beat the dissolved gelatine into the egg yolk mixture. Place in the refrigerator for about 10 minutes, stirring occasionally, until just beginning to set.

5. Meanwhile, whip the cream until it holds soft peaks. Whisk the egg whites in a clean bowl until holding soft peaks. Fold the cream into the egg yolk mixture, then fold in the egg whites. Spoon the soufflé mixture into the chocolate-lined cases and chill until set.

6. To make the sauce, place the reserved passion fruit pulp in a saucepan. Blend the arrowroot into the orange juice and add to the pan. Cook over a high heat, stirring, until boiling and thickened. Leave to cool, stirring occasionally.

7. To serve, remove the foil cups from the ramekins and carefully peel away the foil from the soufflés. Set each soufflé on an individual plate. Pour a little passion fruit sauce on each one and pool the rest of the sauce on the plates. Scatter the reserved seeds in the sauce and serve.

TECHNIQUE

Brush the insides of the foil cups with the melted chocolate, applying an even coating, but leaving the top edge fairly ragged.

WHITE AND DARK CHOCOLATE MOUSSE

This light, yet exceedingly chocolately mousse, with its rich, alternate layers of white and dark, is cut into little towers and sandwiched between thin squares of dark, brittle chocolate, then dusted with cocoa powder. The choice of chocolate is all important – for the most intense flavour, choose one of the best continental brands with a high proportion of cocoa solids.

SERVES 9

225 g (8 oz) plain chocolate

125 g (4 oz) white chocolate

125 g (4 oz) unsalted butter

60 ml (4 tbsp) rum

4 eggs, separated

11 g (0.4 oz) sachet powdered gelatine

300 ml (½ pint) double cream

PREPARATION TIME
45 minutes, plus chilling
COOKING TIME
Nil
FREEZING
Suitable: Stage 3. Thaw overnight in the refrigerator.

510 CALS PER SERVING

1. Line a 15 cm (6 inch) square cake tin with cling film. Set aside half of the plain chocolate. Break up the remaining plain chocolate and the white chocolate and place in separate heatproof bowls. Add half the butter and rum to each bowl and set them over pans of simmering water. Turn off the heat and leave until the chocolate is melted. Add 2 egg yolks to each bowl and stir until smooth.

2. Sprinkle the gelatine over 60 ml (4 tbsp) water in a small heatproof bowl and dissolve over hot water. Whisk the egg whites in a clean bowl until holding soft peaks. Whip the cream in a separate bowl until it holds soft peaks. Divide the cream between the two bowls of chocolate and fold in gently, yet thoroughly. Pour half the dissolved gelatine into each bowl and stir well, then fold half the egg whites into each.

3. Spoon half of the white chocolate mousse mixture into the prepared tin and spread evenly. Carefully spoon half the plain chocolate mixture on top, then repeat the layers of white and plain chocolate; the mixtures will merge slightly. Tap the tin gently on the work surface to level the mousse, then transfer to the refrigerator and leave to set for about 4 hours, or overnight.

4. Melt the remaining chocolate in a small heatproof bowl over a pan of simmering water. Spread out on a sheet of foil to slightly larger than a 15 x 30 cm (6 x 12 inch) rectangle. Leave to set, then trim the edges and cut into 18 squares.

5. To serve, turn out the mousse on to a board lined with cling film and cut into 9 squares, using a sharp knife. Place a square of chocolate underneath each mousse square and top with another chocolate square. Carefully transfer to individual plates and dust with cocoa powder to serve.

TECHNIQUE

Layer the white and dark chocolate mousse mixtures in the prepared tin, spreading each layer evenly with the back of a spoon.

GROUND COFFEE SYLLABUBS

These creamy desserts are flavoured with rich strong coffee. Freshly ground coffee is beaten into cream with sugar and coffee liqueur to give the syllabubs a delightful speckled appearance and a lovely grainy texture. To finish, light frothy vanilla cream is piled on top and dusted, cappuccino-style with a little chocolate powder.

SERVES 6

75-125 g (3-4 oz) caster sugar

300 ml (½ pint) double cream

60 ml (4 tbsp) Kahlua or other coffee liqueur

30 ml (2 tbsp) finely ground coffee

150 ml (¼ pint) whipping cream

10 ml (2 tsp) vanilla sugar (see note on page 12)

30 ml (2 tbsp) drinking chocolate powder

PREPARATION TIME
15 minutes, plus chilling
COOKING TIME
Nil
FREEZING
Not suitable

415 CALS PER SERVING

1. Place the caster sugar, double cream, coffee liqueur, coffee grounds and 60 ml (4 tbsp) water in a large bowl and whisk, using an electric beater or a balloon whisk, until the mixture is thick and floppy and holding a trail from the whisk.

2. Spoon or pour the syllabub mixture into six stemmed glasses – if you have one, pour it through a wide-necked jam funnel to prevent the syllabub touching the sides of the glasses as it goes in. Place the glasses on a tray and set aside in a cool place for 2-3 hours, or place in the refrigerator overnight.

3. Place the whipping cream in a large bowl with the sugar and 60 ml (4 tbsp) ice-cold water and whisk, with an electric beater or a balloon whisk, until thick, light and frothy. Spoon the frothy cream on top of the syllabubs. Dust with chocolate powder and chill until ready to serve.

NOTE: If you prefer to have the syllabub without the coffee grounds, add them to 90 ml (6 tbsp) boiling water and leave to cool, stirring occasionally. Then strain and add to the cream with the liqueur.

Kahlua lends a superb intense flavour. If you use an alternative sweeter coffee liqueur, such as Tia Maria, use the lesser quantity of sugar.

NOTE: If you make this syllabub the day before it is needed the cream and coffee will begin to separate out into two layers, which enhances, rather than detracts from the appearance.

VARIATION

To make a lemon syllabub: Omit the ground coffee and replace the coffee liqueur with medium dry sherry. Add the juice and finely grated rind of 1 lemon to the cream with the sherry and sugar.

TECHNIQUE

Whisk the sugar, cream, coffee, liqueur and water mixture together until the cream is thick enough to hold a trail when the whisk is lifted.

CRÈME FRAÎCHE CRÈMETS WITH RED FRUIT SAUCE

A delicate and delightful blend of tangy cream and soft white cheese set in a pool of tart red sauce. To make the classic heart shape, you'll need special shaped moulds with draining holes which are available from kitchen shops. However, empty, shallow 200 ml (7 fl oz) crème fraîche or yogurt pots make good round substitutes – use a skewer to puncture about eight draining holes in the base of each one.

SERVES 6

300 ml (½ pint) crème
    fraîche
225 g (8 oz) mascarpone
    cheese, or other cream
    cheese
30 ml (2 tbsp) caster sugar
2 egg whites
RED FRUIT SAUCE
25 g (1 oz) blackcurrants
50 g (2 oz) redcurrants
50 g (2 oz) caster sugar
125 g (4 oz) raspberries
TO DECORATE
4 mint sprigs
icing sugar, for dusting
    (optional)

PREPARATION TIME
20 minutes, plus draining
COOKING TIME
3-5 minutes
FREEZING
Not suitable

370 CALS PER SERVING

1. Line six 150 ml (¼ pint) perforated moulds with muslin. Place the crème fraîche, mascarpone cheese and sugar in a large bowl and beat until smooth and light. In a clean bowl, whisk the egg whites until holding soft peaks, then fold into the crème fraîche mixture.

2. Spoon the mixture into the muslin-lined moulds. Place on a tray and leave to drain in a cool place for at least 8 hours, or better still, overnight.

3. To make the sauce, place the black and red currants in a small pan with the sugar, and cook over a low heat for 3-5 minutes until just soft. Press the raspberries through a fine sieve into a bowl, then stir in the black and red currant mixture. Leave to cool.

4. To serve, turn out the crèmets onto individual plates and spoon around the raspberry and currant sauce. Serve at once, decorated with mint sprigs. Dust with a little icing sugar, if desired.

NOTE: Instead of using moulds, you could leave the cream mixture to drain in a large sieve lined with muslin. Serve in small spoonfuls on the fruit sauce.

VARIATION

Lemon-flavoured creams with strawberry sauce are equally good. Add the juice and grated rind of 1 lemon to the cream and cheese. For the sauce, purée 175 g (6 oz) strawberries in a food processor, or push through a fine sieve, then sweeten to taste with 15-30 ml (1-2 tbsp) caster sugar. Spoon the sauce around the crèmets and decorate with a few extra strawberry slices.

TECHNIQUE

Spoon the crème fraîche mixture into the muslin-lined perforated moulds.

LEMON SYLLABUBS WITH GRAPES

Sweet juicy grapes are steeped in a light, lemon-flavoured syrup, then served topped with a frothy syllabub. Choose seedless varieties of grapes and leave them whole. Or if you happen to find the intensely-scented large Muscat grapes, then halve them to reveal their golden flesh and scoop out the seeds with the tip of a teaspoon.

SERVES 6

450 g (1 lb) seedless green
grapes
200 ml (7 fl oz) sweet white
wine
finely pared rind and juice of
1 lemon
45 ml (3 tbsp) caster sugar
300 ml (½ pint) double
cream
TO DECORATE
blanched lemon rind shreds
(see below)

PREPARATION TIME
15 minutes, plus soaking
COOKING TIME
Nil
FREEZING
Not suitable

330 CALS PER SERVING

1. Place the grapes in a bowl with the wine, lemon rind and juice, and the sugar. Stir gently, then leave to macerate for 2-3 hours.

2. Spoon the grapes into tall glasses, then strain the soaking liquid into a bowl. Whip the cream until holding soft peaks, then gradually whisk in the grape liquid until the cream thickens to a floppy consistency.

3. Spoon the syllabub mixture on top of the grapes. Chill for up to 2 hours, or serve at once, decorated with lemon rind shreds.

NOTE: The wine will separate out when the syllabub is left to stand, so if you prefer, serve straight away.

LEMON RIND SHREDS: Finely pare the rind from a small lemon, using a vegetable peeler. Cut into fine strips. Blanch in boiling water for 2 minutes, then drain. Rinse in cold water, drain and dry on kitchen paper.

VARIATION

Replace the grapes with strawberries, halve or quarter them if large and flavour with orange rind and juice instead of lemon.

TECHNIQUE

Gradually whisk the grape soaking liquid into the cream until the mixture thickens to a floppy consistency.

Melon with Summer Fruits

Cubes of scented, pale green and orange melon are tossed with red summer fruits in an orangey, melon sauce to make a delightful fruit salad. A good vanilla ice cream makes an excellent accompaniment. Charentais melon, with its pinky orange flesh, provides colour contrast as well as a superb flavour, although a yellow-fleshed melon could be used instead.

SERVES 4

½ galia or ogen melon

1 charentais melon

150 ml (¼ pint) freshly
    squeezed orange juice

30 ml (2 tbsp) melon liqueur
    or Grand Marnier
    (optional)

125 g (4 oz) strawberries

225 g (8 oz) raspberries

lemon balm sprigs, to
    decorate (optional)

PREPARATION TIME
20 minutes, plus standing
COOKING TIME
Nil
FREEZING
Not suitable

90 CALS PER SERVING

1. Cut the melons into thick wedges, then scoop out the seeds and remove the skin, using a sharp knife. Cut the galia or ogen melon and half of the chanterais melon into cubes and place in a serving bowl.

2. Roughly chop the remaining charentais melon and place in a food processor or blender with the orange juice. Process until smooth. Stir in the liqueur, if using, then pour over the melon cubes.

3. Halve or quarter the strawberries, depending on their size, and add to the melon with the raspberries. Leave at room temperature for at least half an hour to allow the flavours to mingle, before serving.

4. Decorate with lemon balm sprigs if available, then serve accompanied by vanilla ice cream or Greek-style yogurt, if desired.

NOTE: Choose melons that are very ripe. A ripe melon should give slightly to pressure at the stem end. However, if lots of people have already tested the melons in a fruit stall, the melon may be soft through bruising rather than ripeness. So, check the smell too – a ripe melon will be heavily scented.

VARIATION

Omit the raspberries and strawberries from the salad and replace with 2 mangoes. Peel, then cut into 3 wedges around the stone. Cut the mango flesh into cubes, adding any rough shaped pieces to the portion of melon which is to be puréed. Serve with scoops of orange sorbet instead of ice cream.

TECHNIQUE

Halve the melons, then scoop out the seeds from the centre using a tablespoon.

FRUIT SALAD WITH PISTACHIO BISCUITS

Crisp, pistachio nut biscuits are the perfect accompaniment to this refreshing dessert. The fruits suggested below are a particularly good combination, but you can substitute others according to whatever is available. Strawberries, mango, banana (added at the last minute), melon, papaya or grapes could all be used as alternatives.

SERVES 4

2 oranges
5 plums
4 apricots
2 peaches
125 g (4 oz) redcurrants
125 g (4 oz) raspberries
SYRUP
25 g (1 oz) caster sugar
300 ml (½ pint) orange juice
15-30 ml (1-2 tbsp) eau de
  framboise (raspberry
  liqueur), Grand Marnier
  or crème de cassis
  (optional)
PISTACHIO BISCUITS
75 g (3 oz) shelled pistachio
  nuts
75 g (3 oz) unsalted butter
  (at room temperature)
125 g (4 oz) caster sugar
50 g (2 oz) plain flour
30 ml (2 tbsp) milk

PREPARATION TIME
1 hour, plus chilling
COOKING TIME
15-20 minutes
FREEZING
Not suitable

140 CALS PER SERVING

1. First make the pistachio biscuits. Preheat the oven to 200°C (400°F) Mark 6. Line a baking sheet with non-stick baking parchment and grease 2 or 3 rolling pins. Chop the pistachio nuts.

2. Cream the butter and sugar together in a mixing bowl, using an electric beater if possible, until very light and fluffy. Sift in the flour and mix well, then add the milk and beat until smooth. Stir in the pistachio nuts.

3. Place 6 teaspoonfuls of the mixture on the baking sheet, spacing them well apart. Bake for 5-7 minutes until golden brown around the edges. Leave the biscuits to firm up slightly for about 30 seconds, then lift off using a palette knife and place over a rolling pin, pressing gently for a few seconds to curve. When firm, lift off the biscuits and transfer to a wire rack to cool. Bake the remaining mixture in the same way, to make about 18 biscuits.

4. To make the syrup, place the sugar in a saucepan with 100 ml (3½ fl oz) water and dissolve over a low heat, stirring occasionally. Increase the heat and bring the syrup to the boil. Boil rapidly for 2 minutes, then remove from the heat and stir in the orange juice. Add the liqueur if using.

5. Working on a plate to catch the juices, cut the peel and white pith from the oranges using a large sharp knife, then cut out the segments. Halve and stone the plums, apricots and peaches, then cut into thick wedges. Place the fruits in a large glass bowl, together with any juice, and pour over the warm syrup. Chill for up to 2 hours.

6. To finish, stir in the redcurrants and raspberries. Serve at once, accompanied by the pistachio biscuits, and some thick pouring cream if desired.

NOTE: You will only need to serve 2 or 3 pistachio biscuits per person. Store the rest of the biscuits in an airtight tin for another occasion.

TECHNIQUE

Place each soft pistachio biscuit over a rolling pin, then press gently to curve. Leave until firm.

GRILLED PEARS WITH HONEY AND WALNUT ICE CREAM

Ripe pears, poached to a perfect softness in a lemony syrup, are then grilled until just tinged with golden brown. Serve the pears barely warm, drizzled with a little of the syrup and accompanied by a spoonful or two of this nutty, honey-flavoured ice cream. The cool, clear taste of the pears offsets the richness of the ice cream and complements it beautifully.

SERVES 4

4 pears
juice of 1 lemon
300 ml (½ pint) dry Madeira
75 g (3 oz) caster sugar
**HONEY AND WALNUT
   ICE CREAM**
450 ml (¾ pint) double
   cream
½ vanilla pod
4 egg yolks
150 g (5 oz) clear honey
50 g (2 oz) walnuts

PREPARATION TIME
1 hour, plus freezing
COOKING TIME
About 10 minutes
FREEZING
Not suitable

600 CALS PER SERVING

1. First make the ice cream. Pour the cream into a small pan, split the vanilla pod lengthwise and add to the cream. Place over a very low heat and slowly bring to just below boiling point. Whisk the egg yolks in a large bowl until creamy, then pour on the cream, whisking all the time.

2. Return to the pan and cook over a very low heat, stirring continuously, until the custard is just thick enough to coat the back of the spoon. Remove the custard from the heat and stir in the honey. Leave to cool, stirring occasionally to prevent a skin forming.

3. Preheat the oven to 180°C (350°F) Mark 4. Spread out the walnuts on a baking sheet and bake for 15 minutes. Leave to cool, then chop coarsely.

4. When the custard is cold remove the vanilla pod, then stir in the toasted nuts. Transfer to a freezerproof container and freeze for 3-4 hours until firm.

5. Peel the pears, then quarter and core them. Sprinkle with the lemon juice, turning the pears to coat. Pour the Madeira into a large shallow pan, wide enough to take the pears in a single layer, add the sugar and dissolve over a low heat. Increase the heat and boil for 2 minutes, then add the pears and bring to a gentle simmer. Cover the pan and simmer the pears very gently for 4-5 minutes until just tender. Leave to cool in the syrup.

6. Lift the pears out of the syrup and place in a shallow gratin dish. Return the pear syrup to the pan and cook over a high heat until reduced by half. Preheat the grill to high. Pour the syrup over the pears and grill for a few minutes until the pears begin to brown and caramelise. Serve warm, with the ice cream.

NOTE: You will only need to serve about half of the ice cream; keep the rest for another occasion.

TECHNIQUE

Peel, quarter and core the pears, leaving the stalk on one quarter of each pear.

SPICED WINTER FRUIT COMPOTE

Dried fruits are poached in apple and wine syrup – double scented with star anise and cinnamon – then served whole with a dollop of Greek-style yogurt or crème fraîche. Include other dried fruits if you wish – healthfood shops and many larger supermarkets now stock a good variety, especially around Christmas.

SERVES 6

75 g (3 oz) ready-to-eat
    dried pears
75 g (3 oz) ready-to-eat
    dried figs
75 g (3 oz) ready-to-eat
    dried apricots
75 g (3 oz) ready-to-eat
    prunes
300 ml (½ pint) apple juice
    (approximately)
300 ml (½ pint) dry white
    wine
1 star anise
½ cinnamon stick
light muscovado sugar, to
    taste
TO SERVE
150 ml (¼ pint) Greek-style
    yogurt
pinch of ground cinnamon

PREPARATION TIME
10 minutes, plus cooling
COOKING TIME
50 minutes
FREEZING
Suitable

155 CALS PER SERVING

1. Put the dried fruits in a saucepan with 300 ml (½ pint) apple juice, the wine, star anise and cinnamon stick. Place over a low heat and bring slowly to the boil.

2. Reduce the heat, cover the pan and simmer for 45 minutes until the fruits are plump and tender. Check the liquid during cooking to ensure there is sufficient; add a little more apple juice if necessary.

3. Turn the compote into a bowl. Taste the cooking liquid for sweetness, adding a little sugar if necessary. Allow to cool to room temperature.

4. To serve, divide the compote between individual glass dishes. Accompany with crème fraîche or thick Greek yogurt, topped with a light sprinkling of cinnamon.

NOTE: Ready-to-eat dried fruits are already rehydrated slightly, however different varieties soak up more or less liquid during cooking, so it is important to keep a watch and add a little more apple juice, if necessary.

VARIATION

Replace the figs with apple rings and the pears with raisins.

TECHNIQUE

To impart the spicy flavour, add the cinnamon stick and star anise to the dried fruits before cooking.

ROASTED PEACHES WITH PISTACHIO STUFFING

Flavourful fresh peaches are stuffed with a lightly spiced crunchy filling of amaretti biscuit crumbs and pale green pistachios, then baked until softened. A dollop of creamy Greek yogurt or crème fraîche is the perfect complement. For a richer accompaniment, try the Sabayon sauce variation, but be sure to use a good medium dry white wine – Champagne, if you have a glass to spare, strikes just the right balance!

SERVES 6

50 g (2 oz) amaretti biscuits

75 g (3 oz) shelled pistachio nuts

25 g (1 oz) light muscovado sugar

1.25 ml (¼ tsp) Chinese five-spice powder

2 egg yolks

6 peaches (see note)

TO SERVE

Greek-style yogurt or crème fraîche

PREPARATION TIME
15 minutes
COOKING TIME
20 minutes
FREEZING
Not suitable

175 CALS PER SERVING

1. Preheat the oven to 180°C (350°F) Gas 4. Roughly crush the amaretti biscuits between 2 sheets of greaseproof paper, using a rolling pin; or by processing briefly in a food processor. Finely chop the pistachios. Mix the crushed biscuits and pistachios in a bowl with the sugar, spice and egg yolks.

2. Cut the peaches in half and remove the stones. Pile the nut filling into the peach halves and place them in a baking dish. Pour 150 ml (¼ pint) water around the peaches and bake in the oven for 20 minutes or until the peaches are soft.

3. Transfer the stuffed peaches to individual serving plates and serve immediately, accompanied by Greek yogurt or crème fraîche.

NOTE: The cooking time depends very much on the ripeness of the peaches – though if you have a choice, select fruits that are almost, but not quite, ripe enough to eat.

VARIATION

Instead of Greek yogurt, serve the peaches with a sabayon sauce. To make this, put 2 egg yolks, 25 g (1 oz) caster sugar and 60 ml (4 tbsp) medium dry white wine in a large bowl over a pan of barely simmering water and whisk using an electric beater or large balloon whisk for about 10 minutes until the mixture is creamy and frothy.

TECHNIQUE

Spoon the pistachio filling into the peach halves, piling it up well in the middle.

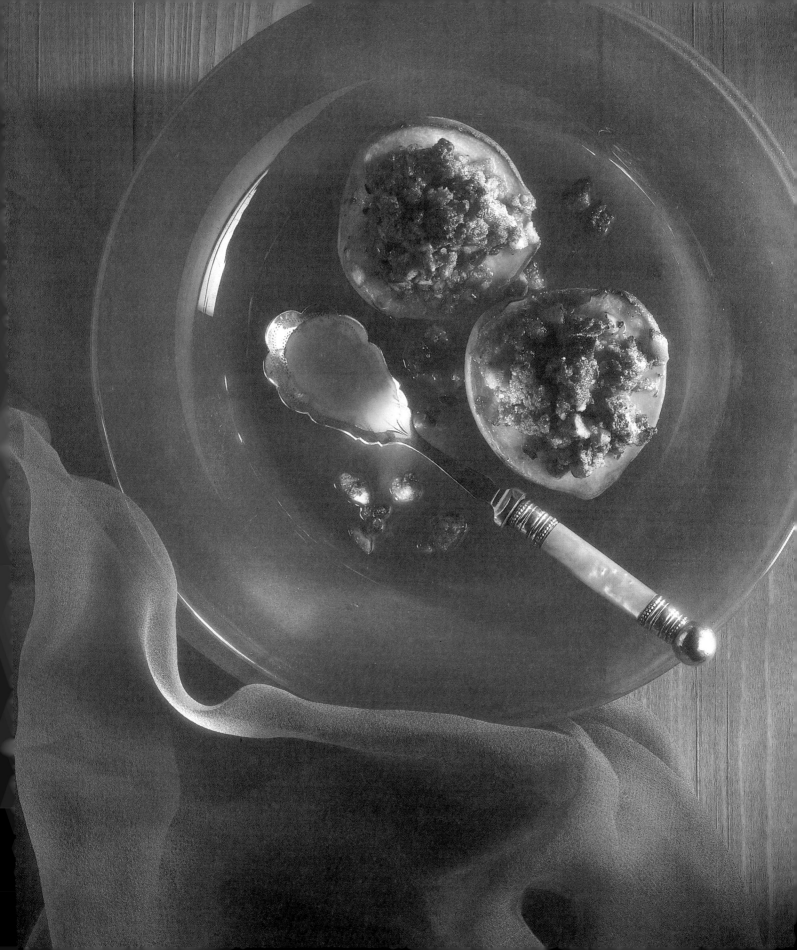

CINNAMON AND HONEY WAFERS WITH RASPBERRIES

Flavourful raspberries are layered with cream and yogurt between rounds of crisp honey and cinnamon wafers, then dusted generously with icing sugar. If you make the biscuits ahead of time, keep them in an airtight tin so they stay crisp. Once the dessert is assembled, serve it within half an hour, or the biscuits will soften.

SERVES 8

CINNAMON WAFERS

50 g (2 oz) unsalted butter (at room temperature)

75 g (3 oz) icing sugar

60 ml (4 tbsp) clear honey

75 g (3 oz) plain flour

5 ml (1 tsp) ground cinnamon

1 egg white, lightly beaten

FILLING

300 ml (½ pint) double cream

150 ml (¼ pint) Greek-style yogurt

30 ml (2 tbsp) icing sugar

30 ml (2 tbsp) framboise (raspberry liqueur) or kirsch (optional)

350-450 g (12 oz-1lb) raspberries

TO DECORATE

icing sugar, for dusting

mint sprigs

PREPARATION TIME
35 minutes, plus cooling
COOKING TIME
20-30 minutes
FREEZING
Suitable: Biscuits only

355 CALS PER SERVING

1. First make the cinnamon wafers. Preheat the oven to 225°C (425°F) Mark 7. Line two large baking sheets with non-stick baking parchment. Beat the butter in a bowl until very soft, then beat in the icing sugar and honey. Sift together the flour and cinnamon and stir into the mixture with the egg white to make a smooth batter.

2. Drop 4-6 heaped teaspoonfuls of the mixture onto the baking sheets, spacing well apart, and spread out to 7.5 cm (3 inch) rounds with the back of the spoon. Bake in the oven for 5-7 minutes until golden, then carefully lift off the baking sheet with a palette knife and transfer to a wire rack to cool and crisp. Use the remaining mixture to make at least 24 wafers in all.

3. To make the filling, whip the cream until holding soft peaks. Fold in the yogurt, sugar and liqueur, if using.

4. To assemble, layer up the wafers in threes, sandwiching them together with the cream and raspberries. Dust generously with icing sugar and serve at once, decorated with mint sprigs.

NOTE: Don't overcrowd the baking sheets, when making the wafers. Spread 4-6 rounds on the baking sheet, keeping them well-spaced apart, so they cook to an even golden colour. It is important that the baking paper is flat, and not creased, otherwise the wafers will form odd shapes as they bake.

VARIATION

Use 225 g (8 oz) strawberries, sliced, and 2 oranges, peeled and segmented, in place of the raspberries. Use Grand Marnier or other orange-flavoured liqueur rather than framboise.

TECHNIQUE

Spread the heaped teaspoonfuls of wafer mixture into 7.5 cm (3 inch) rounds, using the back of the spoon.

FRUIT TERRINE WITH STRAWBERRY SAUCE

This splendid terrine has alternate layers of vivid orange and ruby red jelly set with raspberries and orange segments. A peppery strawberry sauce – flavoured with balsamic vinegar – is the ideal complement.

SERVES 6

300 ml (½ pint) orange juice

300 ml (½ pint) ruby red orange juice

1½ x 11 g (0.4 oz) sachets powdered gelatine

15 ml (1 tbsp) Grand Marnier or other orange-flavoured liqueur

50 g (2 oz) caster sugar

3 oranges

225 g (8 oz) raspberries

SAUCE

225 g (8 oz) strawberries, hulled

50 g (2 oz) caster sugar

10 ml (2 tsp) balsamic vinegar (optional)

5-10 ml (1-2 tsp) freshly ground black pepper

PREPARATION TIME
25 minutes, plus setting
COOKING TIME
Nil
FREEZING
Not suitable

150 CALS PER SERVING

1. Line a 1.2 litre (2 pint) loaf tin with cling film. Pour 45 ml (3 tbsp) of each orange juice into separate small heat-proof bowls. Sprinkle on the gelatine, dividing it equally between them. Leave to soften for a few minutes, then stand the bowls in a pan of hot water until the gelatine has dissolved. Add each gelatine liquid to the appropriate fruit juice.

2. Stir the orange liqueur and half of the sugar into the orange-coloured jelly, then pour half of this into the prepared mould. Scatter over half of the raspberries. Chill until just set.

3. Meanwhile, cut the peel and white pith from the oranges, then cut out the segments. Cut each segment into 2 or 3 pieces; drain in a sieve.

4. When the first layer of orange jelly has just set, arrange the orange segments on top. Stir the remaining sugar into the ruby red orange jelly, pour gently over the orange jelly and chill again until just set.

5. Pour the remaining orange-coloured jelly on top and scatter over the remaining raspberries. Return to the refrigerator and leave to set firmly.

6. To make the strawberry sauce, put the strawberries in a food processor or blender with the sugar, vinegar and pepper, and purée until smooth. Chill until ready to serve.

7. To serve, turn out the terrine onto a board and carefully peel off the cling film. Cut into slices, using a large serrated knife that has been dipped into hot water. Pour the strawberry sauce on to individual plates and arrange a slice or two of the fruit terrine on top.

NOTE: Make sure that each layer of jelly is only just set, before you add the next one: the surface should be slightly sticky. If set too firmly, the layers may not hold together once the terrine is turned out. Keep jelly for subsequent layers at room temperature – place the jugs of jelly in a pan of lukewarm water if they begin to set.

TECHNIQUE

Scatter half of the raspberries over the bottom layer of orange-coloured jelly – they will sink into the jelly as you do so.

SUMMER PUDDING

This quintessential British pudding needs nothing more than a dollop of cream. It uses the most basic of ingredients – white bread – to enclose gleaming red fresh summer fruits, and turns out to be something quite sublime. It's extremely easy to make – and like all great dinner party puddings – is made the night before, ready to turn out and serve when required.

SERVES 6-8

450 g (1 lb) raspberries
225 g (8 oz) redcurrants
225 g (8 oz) blackcurrants
75 g (3 oz) caster sugar
8 large slices white bread,
   5 mm (¼ inch) thick
   (see note)
TO DECORATE
sprigs of redcurrants
lemon balm or mint leaves

PREPARATION TIME
35 minutes, plus chilling
COOKING TIME
5 minutes
FREEZING
Suitable

180-135 CALS PER SERVING

1. Place the raspberries in a saucepan, with the red and black currants, sugar and 45 ml (3 tbsp) water. Bring to a gentle simmer over a low heat, then cook gently for 3-4 minutes until the juices begin to run. Remove from the heat and set aside.

2. Remove the crusts from the bread slices, then cut a round of bread from one slice to fit the base of a 1.5 litre (2½ pint) pudding basin. Cut the remaining slices in half lengthways.

3. Arrange the bread slices around the side of the pudding basin, overlapping them slightly at the bottom, so they fit neatly and tightly together. Position the round of bread to cover the hole in the middle.

4. Spoon about 100 ml (3½ fl oz) of the fruit juice into a jug and set aside. Spoon the remaining fruit and its juice into the bread-lined pudding basin. Cover completely with the remaining bread slices, trimming them to fit as necessary.

5. Cover the pudding with a saucer, that fits just inside the top of the pudding basin, then set a 2 kg (4 lb) weight on the saucer. Chill the pudding in the refrigerator overnight.

6. To serve the pudding, remove the weight and saucer and invert the serving plate over the pudding basin. Hold the two firmly together and turn them over. Give them a firm, shake (up and down, rather than side to side), then lift off the pudding basin.

7. Spoon the reserved juice over the pudding and decorate with redcurrant sprigs and lemon balm or mint sprigs. Serve, cut into wedges, with cream.

NOTE: Choose a good quality close-textured large white loaf, preferably one-day old.

VARIATION

Vary the fruits according to availability. Blackberries, blueberries, cherries and plums are all suitable. Just ensure that the total weight of fruit is 900 g (2 lb).

TECHNIQUE

Line the side of the pudding basin with bread, overlapping the slices slightly at the bottom, to ensure that there are no gaps.

PRUNES IN ARMAGNAC ICE CREAM

Just a hint of cinnamon adds a spicy note to this ice cream, which is speckled with armagnac-plumped prunes. You will need to prepare these prunes at least one month before you want to serve this recipe. Serve the ice cream scooped into glass dishes, with an extra spoonful or two of the prunes and syrup.

SERVES 6

PRUNES IN ARMAGNAC
450 (1 lb) prunes
2 tea bags
175 g (6 oz) caster sugar
300 ml (½ pint) armagnac
ICE CREAM
500 ml (16 fl oz) milk
4 egg yolks
125 g (4 oz) caster sugar
1.25 ml (¼ tsp) ground
   cinnamon
200 ml (7 fl oz) double
   cream

PREPARATION TIME
50 minutes, plus standing and
freezing
COOKING TIME
15-20 minutes
FREEZING
Suitable

660 CALS PER SERVING

1. Place the prunes in a large bowl. Bring 750 ml (1¼ pints) water to the boil, pour into a teapot and add the tea bags. Leave to infuse for 5 minutes, then pour the tea over the prunes, discarding the tea bags. Cover and leave to soak overnight.

2. The following day, place the sugar in a saucepan with 100 ml (3½ fl oz) water. Dissolve over a low heat, stirring occasionally, then bring to the boil. Strain the prunes, place them in a sterilized glass jar and pour over the hot syrup and armagnac. Leave to cool, then cover and leave in a cool place for 1 month.

3. To make the ice cream, pour the milk into a saucepan and bring almost to the boil. Meanwhile whisk the egg yolks, sugar and cinnamon together in a large bowl until foamy. Pour on the hot milk, whisking continuously, then return the mixture to the pan. Cook over a very low heat, stirring all the time with a wooden spoon, until the custard thickens enough to coat the back of the spoon. Pass through a fine sieve, then leave to cool, stirring occasionally.

4. Pour the custard into a freezerproof container, cover and freeze for 2-3 hours until beginning to firm, then transfer to a food processor and process until smooth, or place in a large bowl and beat thoroughly. Beat in the cream and freeze again for 2 hours.

5. Remove the ice cream from the freezer and process or beat again until smooth. Remove 8 prunes from the armagnac, stone them, then add to the processor and whizz until finely chopped. Alternatively chop finely and beat into the ice cream. Freeze again until firm.

6. To serve, scoop the ice cream into serving dishes and add a few prunes in armagnac. Serve at once.

VARIATION

Omit the armagnac, and soak the prunes in the syrup only overnight. Increase the cinnamon to 5 ml (1 tsp).

TECHNIQUE

Beat the chopped armagnac-flavoured prunes into the semi-frozen ice cream.

RASPBERRY AND COCOA SORBETS

This duo of sorbets tastes as exciting as it looks. Dark chocolate makes a quite surprising good sorbet – cocoa is used here to give a wonderfully intense flavour. The refreshing raspberry sorbet provides a fantastic colour and flavour contrast. Crisp dessert biscuits are the perfect accompaniment.

SERVES 6

CHOCOLATE SORBET
40 g (1½ oz) cocoa powder
100 g (3½ oz) granulated sugar
5 ml (1 tsp) vanilla essence
1 egg white
RASPBERRY SORBET
450 g (1 lb) raspberries
175 g (6 oz) caster sugar
juice of 2 lemons
1 egg white
TO FINISH
125 g (4 oz) raspberries
lemon balm or mint leaves, to decorate
icing sugar, for dusting

PREPARATION TIME
40 minutes, plus freezing
COOKING TIME
5 minutes
FREEZING
Suitable

230 CALS PER SERVING

1. To make the chocolate sorbet, place the cocoa powder, sugar and 450 ml (¾ pint) water in a heavy-based saucepan. Dissolve over a low heat, stirring occasionally, then bring to the boil and boil for 2 minutes, without stirring. Remove from the heat, stir in the vanilla essence and leave to cool.

2. Pour the cocoa mixture into a freezer-proof container and freeze for 2-3 hours until slushy. Whisk the egg white until holding soft peaks. Whizz the sorbet in a food processor, or tip into a bowl and beat well, then fold in the egg white. Return to the freezer container, cover and freeze for 3-4 hours until firm.

3. To make the raspberry sorbet, place the sugar in a saucepan with 150 ml (¼ pint) water and dissolve over a low heat, stirring occasionally, then bring to the boil and boil for 2 minutes, without stirring.

4. Whizz the raspberries in a food processor or blender, add the syrup and process again, then sieve to remove the pips. Add the lemon juice and leave to cool. Pour into a freezerproof container, then freeze for 2-3 hours until slushy. Whisk the egg white until holding soft peaks. Briefly process or beat the sorbet, then fold in the egg white. Return to container, cover and freeze until firm.

5. To serve, transfer the sorbets to the refrigerator for 20 minutes to soften, then arrange quenelles of alternate flavours on individual serving plates. Scatter with raspberries and lemon balm or mint leaves. Dust with icing sugar and serve at once.

VARIATION

Use 10 passion fruit in place of the raspberries. Scoop out the pulp and place in a saucepan with 30 ml (2 tbsp) water. Cook over a low heat for 5 minutes, then push through a fine sieve. Substitute oranges for the lemons and continue from step 4.

TECHNIQUE

Whizz the partially frozen sorbet in a food processor to break down the ice crystals.

TOFFEE TRUFFLE BOMBES WITH CARAMEL BANANAS

Toffee and bananas are a terrific taste combination. Here the toffee is made into a gorgeous, golden ice cream, packed into little cups, then filled with a rich chocolate ganache. The icy bombes are turned out, topped with cracked toffee, drizzled with dark melted chocolate and served with hot caramelised bananas.

SERVES 6

TOFFEE ICE CREAM
150 g (5 oz) toffees
150 ml (¼ pint) milk
150 ml (¼ pint) double
  cream
75 g (3 oz) natural fromage
  frais
CHOCOLATE GANACHE
150 ml (¼ pint) double
  cream
150 g (5 oz) plain chocolate
CARAMELISED BANANAS
4 small ripe bananas
30 ml (2 tbsp) light
  muscovado sugar
TO FINISH
50 g (2 oz) plain chocolate,
  melted

PREPARATION TIME
50 minutes, plus freezing
COOKING TIME
3-5 minutes
FREEZING
Suitable: Bombes only

620 CALS PER SERVING

1. To make the ice cream, place the toffees in the freezer for 30 minutes, then cut into small chunks. Set aside 50 g (2 oz). Place the rest in a saucepan with the milk over a low heat, stirring occasionally, until the toffee has melted. Allow to cool, stirring occasionally, then chill.

2. Whip the cream until holding soft peaks, then stir in the fromage frais and chilled toffee mixture. Beat lightly until smooth, then spoon into a freezerproof container, cover and freeze for 3-4 hours until firm. Place six 125 ml (4 fl oz) individual metal pudding basins or freezerproof cups in the freezer to chill.

3. Remove ice cream from freezer and beat well with a wooden spoon, then divide between the moulds. Spread it evenly up the sides of each mould, leaving a hollow in the centre. Freeze for 30 minutes until firm.

4. To make the ganache, place the cream in a saucepan and bring to the boil. Meanwhile, chop the chocolate into small pieces. Remove the cream from the heat, add the chocolate and leave undisturbed for 5 minutes. Stir to a smooth cream, then chill until thickened. Beat lightly, then fill the centre of the toffee bombes with the ganache and level the tops. Freeze for 1 hour until firm.

5. Peel the bananas and cut them at a sharply oblique angle to make long oval 5 mm (¼ inch) thick slices. Spread in a frying pan and sprinkle with the sugar.

6. To serve, dip the moulds in hot water for a few seconds only, then turn out the bombes on to cold plates. Scatter the reserved toffee on top, then drizzle over the melted chocolate, from the end of a spoon. Return the bombes to the freezer to firm up while you sauté the bananas for 3-5 minutes until browned and tender. Spoon the bananas on to the plates and serve at once.

NOTE: If you make the bombes well ahead, transfer to the refrigerator 20 minutes before serving to soften slightly.

TECHNIQUE

Spread the toffee ice cream evenly up the sides of each mould, leaving a space in the centre for the ganache.

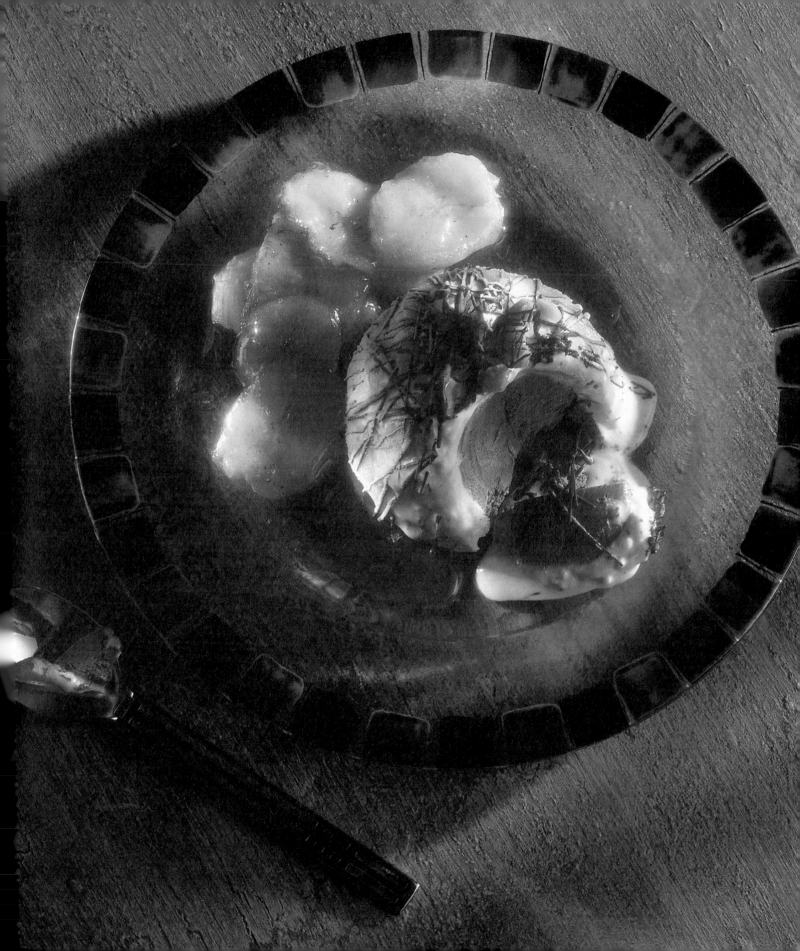

RHUBARB PARFAIT WITH STEM GINGER

Rhubarb, ginger and orange complement each other beautifully in this dessert. Fresh rhubarb is flavoured with a hint of orange and puréed to mix with cream and custard for a softly frozen parfait. Finely diced ginger adds little bursts of flavour as you eat. Serve the parfait with crisp dessert biscuits.

SERVES 8

200 ml (7 fl oz) milk
finely pared rind of 1 orange
4 egg yolks
150 g (5 oz) caster sugar
450 g (1 lb) rhubarb
30 ml (2 tbsp) orange juice
250 ml (8 fl oz) double
　cream
TO SERVE
2-3 pieces preserved stem
　ginger in syrup
150 ml (¼ pint) crème
　fraîche or Greek-style
　yogurt

PREPARATION TIME
40 minutes, plus freezing
COOKING TIME
About 20 minutes
FREEZING
Suitable

225 CALS PER SERVING

1. Line a 1 litre (1¾ pint) loaf tin with cling film. Pour the milk into a saucepan, add the orange rind and slowly bring to the boil over a very low heat. Meanwhile, place the egg yolks and sugar in a large bowl and whisk together until pale and creamy. Pour the milk on to the egg yolk mixture, whisking all the time, then strain back into the pan.

2. Cook the custard over a low heat, stirring constantly, until it thickens enough to coat the back of the spoon; do not boil. Remove from the heat, pour into a large bowl and cool, stirring occasionally. Cover the surface closely with dampened greaseproof paper to prevent a skin forming; leave until cold.

3. Trim the rhubarb stalks, cut into short lengths and place in a saucepan with the orange juice. Cover and cook over a low heat for 5-7 minutes until the rhubarb is soft. Purée in a food processor or blender, or beat well until smooth. Transfer to a bowl and leave to cool.

4. When the rhubarb and custard are both cold, whip the cream until it holds soft peaks, then fold into the rhubarb purée with the custard. Pour the rhubarb mixture into the prepared loaf tin. Cover with cling film and freeze for at least 6 hours, or overnight.

5. About 20 minutes before serving, transfer the rhubarb parfait to the refrigerator to soften slightly. Shred half of the preserved stem ginger; finely chop the remainder. Fold the chopped ginger into the crème fraîche or yogurt. Turn the rhubarb parfait out on to a cling-film lined board. Cut into slices and arrange on chilled serving plates. Sprinkle with the shredded ginger and serve at once, with a spoonful of the ginger-flavoured cream or yogurt.

VARIATION

Replace the rhubarb with plums. Halve and stone the plums, then cook until tender and push through a sieve to remove the skins.

TECHNIQUE

Lightly fold the whipped cream and cooled custard into the rhubarb mixture, using a large spatula.

CLEMENTINE ICE CREAM WITH RUBY ORANGE SAUCE

Thin wedges of citrus ice cream, wrapped in a dark chocolate sponge crust, are served on a vibrant ruby red orange sauce. If ruby red orange juice is not available, use ordinary orange juice instead.

SERVES 8

CLEMENTINE ICE CREAM
250 ml (8 fl oz) milk
4 egg yolks
125 g (4 oz) caster sugar
grated rind and juice of 6
 clementines
300 ml (½ pint) double
 cream

CHOCOLATE CRUST
1 egg, plus 1 egg yolk
50 g (2 oz) light muscovado
 sugar
45 ml (3 tbsp) plain flour
15 ml (1 tbsp) cocoa powder
20 g (¾ oz) butter, melted
 and cooled

ORANGE SAUCE
2 oranges
450 ml (¾ pint) ruby red
 orange juice
125 g (4 oz) caster sugar
15 ml (1 tbsp) arrowroot,
 blended with 15 ml (1 tbsp)
 water

PREPARATION TIME
1¼ hours, plus freezing
COOKING TIME
10-12 minutes
FREEZING
Suitable: Except sauce

470 CALS PER SERVING

1. First make the ice cream. Heat the milk in a saucepan until almost boiling. Meanwhile, whisk the egg yolks and sugar together in a large bowl until thick and creamy. Whisk in the hot milk, then return to the pan and cook, stirring, over a low heat, until thick enough to coat the back of the spoon. Strain into a large bowl. Add the clementine rind and juice. Leave to cool, stirring occasionally.

2. Whip the cream until holding soft peaks, then fold into the custard. Transfer to a freezerproof container, cover and freeze for 2-3 hours until just firm.

3. Preheat the oven to 190°C (375°F) Mark 5. Grease and line a 20 x 30 cm (8 x 12 inch) Swiss roll tin. Line a 20 cm (8 inch) round spring-release cake tin with cling film.

4. To make the chocolate crust, whisk the egg, egg yolk and sugar in a large bowl over a pan of barely simmering water until the mixture is thick and foamy and will hold a trail.

5. Sift in the flour and cocoa and pour in the butter around the edge. Fold in gently, then pour into the Swiss roll tin and spread evenly. Bake for 10-12 minutes until springy to the touch. Turn out onto a sheet of sugared greaseproof paper and cut out a 20 cm (8 inch) round.

6. Place the round in the cake tin, crust side down. Cut four 2.5 cm (1 inch) strips and use to line the side of the tin, trimming to fit as necessary. Leave to cool.

7. Remove ice cream from freezer and beat thoroughly. Spread in the tins; cover and freeze for 1-2 hours until firm.

8. To make the sauce, pare the rind from 1 orange, shred finely and place in a saucepan with the orange juice and sugar. Dissolve over a low heat, then increase heat and cook for 3 minutes. Stir in the arrowroot and cook, stirring for 1-2 minutes, until thickened. Cool, stirring occasionally. Peel and segment the oranges, discarding all pith, then add to the sauce.

9. Serve the ice cream cut into thin wedges, with the sauce.

TECHNIQUE

Line the side of the tin with the chocolate cake strips, crust-side out, to fit snugly.

ICED HAZELNUT MOUSSES WITH WARM SPICED PLUMS

Tart plums are cooked until just tender in a lightly spiced citrus syrup to serve with creamy iced hazelnut mousses, which are set in little oval or round moulds. Don't serve the mousses too cold: if you make them well ahead, transfer to the refrigerator about 15 minutes before serving to soften.

SERVES 6

75 g (3 oz) hazelnuts
75 g (3 oz) caster sugar
3 egg whites
125 g (4 oz) icing sugar
300 ml (½ pint) double
 cream
SPICED PLUMS
700 g (1½ lb) plums
125 g (4 oz) light muscovado
 sugar
5 ml (2 tsp) Chinese five-
 spice powder
grated rind and juice of
 1 orange
grated rind of 1 lemon

PREPARATION TIME
40 minutes, plus freezing
COOKING TIME
2-3 minutes
FREEZING
Suitable: Mousses only

565 CALS PER SERVING

1. Grease a baking sheet. Place the hazelnuts, caster sugar and 30 ml (2 tbsp) water in a small pan over a low heat until the sugar has dissolved. Increase the heat and cook until the syrup turns a deep caramel colour. Immediately tip the nut mixture out on to the baking sheet and leave to cool. When cold break up the nut mixture and briefly process in a food processor until coarsely ground, or crush using a rolling pin. Set aside.

2. Place the egg whites and icing sugar in a large bowl over a pan of barely simmering water and whisk using an electric beater or a balloon whisk until thick. Remove the bowl from the heat and continue whisking until the meringue is cool and holding soft peaks.

3. Whip the cream in a separate bowl until floppy and fold into the meringue, together with the ground nut mixture. Rinse out six 150 ml (¼ pint) oval moulds or ramekins with cold water, then divide the hazelnut mixture between them. Smooth the tops, cover and freeze for 2-3 hours until form.

4. To prepare the spiced plums, halve, stone and slice the plums, then place in a saucepan with the sugar, spice, orange juice and orange and lemon rinds. Bring to the boil, then reduce the heat, cover

and simmer gently for 2-3 minutes until the plums are only just tender. Set aside for 10-15 minutes.

5. To serve, dip the moulds or ramekins in very hot water for a few seconds only, then turn out the iced mousses on to cold plates. Spoon around the warm plums and serve at once.

NOTE: Chinese five-spice powder is a blend of anise powder, cinnamon, fennel, star anise and cloves.

VARIATION

Replace the caster sugar and hazelnuts with 175 g (6 oz) amaretti biscuits. Process or grind coarsely, then add to the meringue with the cream.

TECHNIQUE

Carefully turn the hazelnut praline mixture on to the greased baking sheet.

ICED GINGER AND WHITE CHOCOLATE CAKE

Gingercake crumbs form the basis of a light parfait, which is layered and topped with a tumble of white chocolate ganache, then served dusted liberally with a mixture of cocoa and icing sugar. Chocolate ganache, a mixture of melted chocolate and cream, is simple to prepare – just make sure that it has cooled and thickened sufficiently to pipe, otherwise it won't hold its shape.

SERVES 8

CHOCOLATE GANACHE
300 g (10 oz) white
   chocolate, in pieces
300 ml (½ pint) double
   cream
GINGER PARFAIT
125 g (4 oz) ready-made
   gingerbread
450 ml (¾ pint) double
   cream
125 g (4 oz) caster sugar
4 egg yolks
finely grated rind and juice
   of 1 orange
TO FINISH
15 ml (1 tbsp) icing sugar
15 ml (1 tbsp) cocoa powder

PREPARATION TIME
50 minutes, plus freezing
COOKING TIME
3-4 minutes
FREEZING
Suitable

785 CALS PER SERVING

1. Line a 20 cm (8 inch) spring-release round cake tin with non-stick baking parchment. To make the chocolate ganache, put the chocolate in a large bowl. Bring the cream to the boil in a small pan, then pour onto the chocolate and leave to stand for 5 minutes. Using a large balloon whisk, beat the mixture until smooth. Chill until thick.

2. To make the parfait, crumble the gingerbread in a food processor, or into a bowl using your fingers. Add 150 ml (¼ pint) cream and process until smooth, or beat well. Place in the refrigerator.

3. Put the sugar and 125 ml (4 fl oz) water in a saucepan over a low heat, stirring occasionally, until the sugar has dissolved. Increase the heat and boil steadily for 2-3 minutes. Working quickly, place the egg yolks in a large bowl and, whisk in the syrup, in a steady stream. Continue whisking until the mixture is cold and very thick.

4. Whip the remaining cream in a bowl, and fold into the ginger mixture with the orange juice and rind. Fold in the egg yolk mixture. Freeze the parfait mixture for 30 minutes until semi-firm. Spoon half into the prepared tin and smooth the surface.

5. Beat the chocolate ganache lightly until smooth, then put into a large piping bag fitted with a 5 mm (¼ inch) plain nozzle. Pipe half of the ganache in a tumbling, curly pattern over the ginger parfait; it should sink in slightly. Spoon over the remaining ginger parfait, spread evenly, then pipe the remaining chocolate ganache on top in the same way.

6. Cover the tin with cling film or foil and freeze for 3-4 hours until firm. About 20 minutes before serving, unclip the tin, peel off the paper carefully and transfer the cake to a serving plate. Dust liberally with icing sugar and cocoa powder and place in the refrigerator until required. Serve cut into wedges.

TECHNIQUE

Pipe the white chocolate ganache over the ginger parfait in long trails, forming a tumbling, curly pattern.

SAFFRON MERINGUES WITH BLUEBERRY SAUCE

Crisp meringues, flavoured with the merest hint of saffron, are sandwiched with crème fraîche to serve with a richly coloured, mint-scented blueberry sauce. The chunky sauce is based on the Russian Kissel and can be made with any number of summer fruits – you could try cherries, raspberries, strawberries and red- or blackcurrants.

SERVES 6

MERINGUES
small pinch of saffron threads (optional)
2 egg whites
125 g (4 oz) caster sugar
200 ml (7 fl oz) crème fraîche
BLUEBERRY SAUCE
450 g (1 lb) blueberries
40 g (1½ oz) caster sugar
30 ml (2 tbsp) chopped fresh mint

PREPARATION TIME
25 minutes
COOKING TIME
2 hours
FREEZING
Suitable

260 CALS PER SERVING

1. Preheat the oven to 110°C (225°F) Mark ¼. Line two baking sheets with non-stick baking parchment. Put the saffron (if using) in a small bowl and pour on 15 ml (1 tbsp) boiling water. Whisk the egg whites in a large bowl until holding soft peaks. Whisk in 30 ml (2 tbsp) of the sugar, then strain in the saffron liquid and whisk again until the meringue is stiff. Fold in the remaining sugar.

2. Using two large spoons, shape the meringue mixture into 12 oval mounds on the prepared baking sheets. Bake in the oven for about 2 hours until the meringues are well dried out. If using a conventional (rather than fan-assisted) oven, switch the baking sheets around halfway through cooking. Carefully peel the meringues off the paper and leave to cool on a wire rack.

3. To make the sauce, place the blueberries in a saucepan with the sugar and 45 ml (3 tbsp) water and cook over a low heat for 5-7 minutes until they are just tender, but still holding their shape. Using a slotted spoon, remove about one quarter of the blueberries and press through a fine sieve into a large bowl. Stir in the rest of the blueberries with the chopped mint and leave to cool, stirring occasionally.

4. About 1 hour before serving, sandwich the meringues together with the crème fraîche. Pile on to one or two serving dishes, cover and chill until ready to serve. Pour the sauce into a jug and serve with the meringues.

NOTE: Meringues can be made well ahead. Store in an airtight container until ready to use.

VARIATION

Omit the saffron, and add 5 ml (1 tsp) ground cinnamon to the egg whites with the sugar. Replace the blueberries with 450 g (1 lb) mixed summer fruits. In the winter use frozen soft fruits.

TECHNIQUE

Using two large spoons, shape the meringue into large ovals and place on the lined baking sheet.

SQUIDGY CINNAMON MERINGUE CAKE

Really a Pavlova in disguise, this meringue – with its marshmallowy middle – is flavoured with cinnamon and baked in rectangles, then sandwiched together with cream and fromage frais tossed with chunks of fresh strawberries. It is better assembled an hour or two in advance and allowed to soften slightly. Serve in slices in a pool of cassis-flavoured strawberry sauce.

SERVES 8

MERINGUE
3 egg whites
175 g (6 oz) caster sugar
5 ml (1 tsp) cornflour
2.5 ml (½ tsp) ground cinnamon
5 ml (1 tsp) lemon juice
FILLING
200 ml (7 fl oz) double cream
75 g (3 oz) fromage frais
20 ml (4 tsp) vanilla sugar (see note on page 12)
350 g (12 oz) strawberries
STRAWBERRY SAUCE
450 g (1 lb) strawberries
60 ml (4 tbsp) caster sugar
60 ml (4 tbsp) crème de cassis liqueur (optional)
TO FINISH
a little ground cinnamon, for dusting

PREPARATION TIME
30 minutes
COOKING TIME
50 minutes
FREEZING
Suitable

300 CALS PER SERVING

1. Preheat the oven to 150°C (300°F) Mark 2. Line two baking sheets with non-stick baking parchment. Draw three 11 x 23 cm (4½ x 9 inch) rectangles on the paper then turn the paper over so the pencil marks are underneath.

2. Place the egg whites in a large bowl and whisk with an electric beater or large balloon whisk until very stiff. Whisk in the sugar 30 ml (2 tbsp) at a time, whisking well after each addition until the meringue is stiff and shiny. When all the sugar is incorporated, whisk in the cornflour, cinnamon and lemon juice.

3. Pipe or spoon the meringue mixture on to the rectangles on the prepared baking sheets and spread out to fill them evenly. Place in the oven, reduce the temperature to 140°C (275°F) Mark 1 and bake for 50 minutes. Turn off the oven and leave the meringues in the oven until cold.

4. To make the strawberry sauce, either whizz the strawberries in a food processor or blender, then sieve to remove the pips; or simply push them through a fine sieve. Stir in the sugar and liqueur (if using) and chill in the refrigerator until ready to serve.

5. To finish, remove the meringues from the baking sheets, carefully peeling off the paper. For the filling, whip the cream until holding soft peaks and fold into the fromage frais with the vanilla sugar. Chop the strawberries and fold gently into the cream mixture. Sandwich the meringues together with the strawberry mixture, then dust the top with a little cinnamon. Serve, cut into slices, on a pool of the strawberry sauce.

NOTE: If you have a fan-assisted oven, the meringues should bake quite evenly. However in a conventional oven you should switch the baking sheets around halfway through cooking to ensure the meringues cook evenly.

TECHNIQUE

Sandwich the meringue rectangles together with the strawberry cream mixture.

RASPBERRY MOUSSE GÂTEAU

Moist hazelnut sponge rounds are layered with softly whipped cream, tangy raspberry mousse and fresh raspberries. The gâteau is topped with a crown of cream quenelles, toasted nuts and more raspberries.

SERVES 6-8

HAZELNUT CAKE
175 g (6 oz) shelled
  hazelnuts
4 eggs
125 g (4 oz) light muscovado
  sugar
125 g (4 oz) plain flour
2.5 ml (½ tsp) baking
  powder
25 g (1 oz) butter, melted
  and cooled

FILLING AND TOPPING
450 g (1 lb) raspberries
1 egg, separated
25 g (1 oz) caster sugar
7.5 ml (1½ tsp) powdered
  gelatine
450 ml (¾ pint) double
  cream
150 ml (¼ pint) Greek-style
  yogurt

PREPARATION TIME
1½ hours
COOKING TIME
30-35 minutes
FREEZING
Suitable

845-630 CALS PER SERVING

1. Preheat the oven to 180°C (350°F) Mark 4. Grease and base line a 20 cm (8 inch) round cake tin. Spread out the hazelnuts on a baking sheet and bake for 15-20 minutes until browned. Leave to cool, then roughly chop 25 g (1 oz) and set aside. Whizz the rest in a food processor or blender until finely ground.

2. Whisk the eggs and sugar in a large bowl over a pan of barely simmering water until the mixture is thick and pale and will hold a trail. Remove bowl from heat and whisk for a further 3 minutes. Sift flour and baking powder together and fold into the mixture alternately with the ground hazelnuts and melted butter.

3. Spread the mixture in the prepared tin and bake for 30-35 minutes until risen and firm to the touch. Turn out, remove paper and cool on a wire rack.

4. To make the mousse filling, rub half the raspberries through a sieve. Whisk the egg yolk, sugar and raspberry purée in a large bowl over a pan of barely simmering water until the mixture is thick and foamy and will hold a trail. Remove bowl from heat and continue whisking until the mixture is cold.

5. Sprinkle the gelatine over 30 ml (2 tbsp) water in a small heatproof bowl and leave to swell, then stand the bowl in a pan of hot water until the gelatine is dissolved. Meanwhile, whip 50 ml (2 fl oz) cream and fold into the raspberry mixture. Gently stir in the gelatine. Whisk the egg white until holding soft peaks, then fold into the mixture.

6. Line a 20 cm (8 inch) spring-release cake tin with cling film. Cut the hazelnut cake into 3 rounds and trim to a 20 cm (8 inch) diameter. Place one sponge round in the base of the tin. Whip 150 ml (¼ pint) cream and fold in the yogurt, then spread over the cake. Scatter over one third of the reserved raspberries and cover with a second sponge round. Spoon on the mousse, scatter over another third of the raspberries and cover with the remaining sponge. Press down gently, then chill for 2 hours or until the mousse is set.

7. To serve, carefully transfer to a serving plate. Whip the remaining cream and spoon oval mounds around the edge of the cake. Scatter the reserved raspberries and chopped nuts in the middle.

TECHNIQUE

Spoon the raspberry mousse evenly over the second sponge round in the lined tin.

CHOCOLATE MARQUISE

Rich and extremely chocolately, this soft, smooth-textured mousse is poured over a crisp chocolate biscuit base, then chilled until set. Make sure that your refrigerator is turned to its coldest setting, otherwise the mousse won't be firm enough to slice. If it seems just a touch too soft, then pop the mousse in the freezer for 30 minutes before cutting.

SERVES 8

BISCUIT BASE

175 g (6 oz) bourbon or
    chocolate wholemeal
    biscuits

50 g (2 oz) butter

CHOCOLATE MOUSSE

175 g (6 oz) plain chocolate

45 ml (3 tbsp) strong black
    coffee

50 g (2 oz) unsalted butter

15 ml (1 tbsp) whisky

3 eggs

125 g (4 oz) caster sugar

TO FINISH

45 ml (3 tbsp) cocoa powder

white chocolate curls (see
    right-optional)

PREPARATION TIME
25 minutes
COOKING TIME
Nil
FREEZING
Suitable

430 CALS PER SERVING

1. Grease and line a 23 cm (9 inch) spring-release round cake tin. Crush the biscuits coarsely in a polythene bag using a rolling pin, or whizz briefly in a food processor. Melt the butter in a saucepan and stir into the biscuit crumbs, until evenly blended. Spoon the mixture into the prepared tin and press into an even layer. Set aside.

2. To make the mousse topping, break up the chocolate and place in a heatproof bowl with the coffee, butter and whisky. Place the bowl over a pan of hot water and leave to melt. Place the egg yolks and sugar in a large bowl over a pan of barely simmering water and whisk, using an electric beater or balloon whisk, until the mixture is thick and foamy and will hold a trail from the whisk.

3. Whisk the egg whites in a clean bowl until holding soft peaks. Fold the chocolate mixture into the whisked egg yolk mixture, then lightly stir in one third of the egg whites. Fold in the rest and pour into the prepared tin. Spread evenly, then cover and chill in the refrigerator overnight.

4. To serve, unclip the spring-release tin and peel away the lining paper. Carefully transfer the marquise to a serving plate and decorate with white chocolate curls, if preferred. Dust liberally with cocoa powder to serve.

NOTE: When you are making the crumbs for the base, don't process them too finely, otherwise the base will be dense and hard.

CHOCOLATE CURLS: Melt about 75 g (3 oz) white chocolate in a bowl over a pan of hot water. Spread out thinly on a marble slab or clean work surface and leave to set until no longer sticky to the touch. Holding a large knife at a slight angle to the surface, push the blade across the chocolate to shave off long thin curls. Adjust the angle of the blade to obtain the best curls.

TECHNIQUE

Lightly fold the whisked egg whites into the chocolate mixture, using a large spatula or metal spoon.

ALMOND AND AMARETTI CHEESECAKE

A light, creamy cheesecake mixture is encased in a crumbly, crunchy almond case and topped with crushed amaretti biscuits. Make the cheesecake a day before you need it – the texture improves on keeping. Serve a fruity accompaniment – nectarines poached in sweetened red or white wine are perfect.

SERVES 8

BASE

75 g (3 oz) butter

125 g (4 oz) digestive
  biscuits

25 g (1 oz) blanched
  almonds

FILLING

125 g (4 oz) mascarpone
  cheese

125 g (4 oz) ricotta cheese

50 g (2 oz) caster sugar

2 eggs, separated

2.5 ml (½ tsp) vanilla
  essence

15 ml (1 tbsp) cornflour

100 ml (3½ fl oz) crème
  fraîche

TOPPING

50 g (2 oz) amaretti biscuits

NECTARINE COMPOTE

4 ripe nectarines

150 ml (¼ pint) wine

75 g (3 oz) caster sugar

1 vanilla pod

PREPARATION TIME
35 minutes
COOKING TIME
1½ hours
FREEZING
Not suitable

445 CALS PER SERVING

1. Preheat the oven to 150°C (300°F) Mark 2. Grease and line a 20 cm (8 inch) loose-based or springform cake tin. Melt the butter in a small pan. Meanwhile, whizz the biscuits and almonds in a food processor, or crush the biscuits using a rolling pin and chop the almonds finely, then mix into the butter.

2. Spread the biscuit mixture over the base and about 1 cm (½ inch) up the side of the tin, pressing it firmly with the back of a spoon. Set aside.

3. Place the mascarpone and ricotta cheeses in a large bowl and beat together well. Add the sugar, egg yolks, vanilla essence and cornflour and beat again, then fold in the crème fraîche. Whisk the egg whites until holding soft peaks. Stir one third of the egg whites into the cheesecake mixture, then carefully fold in the rest.

4. Pour the mixture into the prepared tin. Crumble the amaretti biscuit into chunky crumbs and scatter over the top. Bake in the oven, just below the middle, for 1½ hours until just firm to the touch. Turn off the heat and leave the cheesecake to cool in the oven.

5. Meanwhile, make the nectarine compote. Halve the nectarines, remove the

stones, then cut into quarters and place in a saucepan with the wine, sugar, vanilla pod and 150 ml (¼ pint) water. Bring slowly to the boil, then reduce the heat, cover and simmer very gently for about 5 minutes until the nectarines are just tender. Allow to cool, then discard the vanilla pod and chill in the refrigerator for several hours.

6. Serve the cheesecake, cut into wedges, with the compote.

NOTE: If mascarpone and/or ricotta are not available, substitute cream cheese and curd cheese respectively.

TECHNIQUE

Press the biscuit mixture evenly over the base and about 1 cm (½ inch) up the side of the tin, using the back of a spoon.

CHOCOLATE ROULADE WITH RED FRUIT COMPOTE

This classic dark roulade is filled with lightly sweetened cream and fromage frais, scattered with red and black soft fruits and served in thick slices with a flavourful summer fruit compote. Don't worry if the roulade cracks slightly as you roll it, the cracks are part of its charm!

SERVES 8-10

ROULADE

125 g (4 oz) plain chocolate, in pieces

4 eggs, separated

125 g (4 oz) caster sugar

30 ml (2 tbsp) cocoa powder, sifted

FILLING

200 ml (7 fl oz) double cream

90 ml (3 fl oz) plain fromage frais

30 ml (2 tbsp) icing sugar

RED FRUIT COMPOTE

250 g (9 oz) blackberries

50 g (2 oz) caster sugar

150 g (5 oz) redcurrants

225 g (8 oz) raspberries

30 ml (2 tbsp) crème de cassis liqueur (optional)

TO SERVE

icing sugar, for dusting

PREPARATION TIME
40 minutes
COOKING TIME
20 minutes
FREEZING
Suitable

390-315 CALS PER SERVING

1. Preheat the oven to 180°C (350°F) Mark 4. Grease and line a 23 x 33 cm (9 x 13 inch) Swiss roll tin.

2. To make the roulade, melt the chocolate in a heatproof bowl over a pan of hot water. Stir, then leave to cool slightly. Meanwhile, whisk the egg yolks and sugar in a large bowl over a pan of barely simmering water until very thick and creamy. Beat in the chocolate.

3. Whisk the egg whites in a bowl until holding stiff peaks, then carefully fold into the chocolate mixture with the cocoa. Pour into the prepared tin and spread evenly. Bake for about 20 minutes until well risen and firm to the touch.

4. While the roulade is cooking, sprinkle a sheet of greaseproof paper generously with caster sugar. Turn out the roulade on to the paper and peel off the lining paper. Cover with a damp tea-towel and leave to cool.

5. To make the compote, place the blackberries and sugar in a small pan and cook over a low heat for 5-8 minutes until just soft. Remove from heat, add the redcurrants and allow to cool.

6. When cold, transfer one third of the fruit to a bowl, using a slotted spoon.

Add 50 g (2 oz) of the raspberries and set aside for the filling. Press the remaining raspberries through a nylon sieve and stir into the fruit compote in the pan, with the liqueur (if using).

7. When the roulade is cold, make the filling. Whip the cream until holding soft peaks and fold in the fromage frais and icing sugar. Carefully spread over the roulade, then scatter over the fruit filling. Roll up from one of the narrow ends, using the paper to help.

8. Transfer the roulade to a board and dust generously with the icing sugar. Spoon the red fruit compote on to individual plates. Cut the roulade into slices and arrange on the compote.

TECHNIQUE

Turn the roulade out on to a sheet of sugared greaseproof paper. Carefully remove the lining paper.

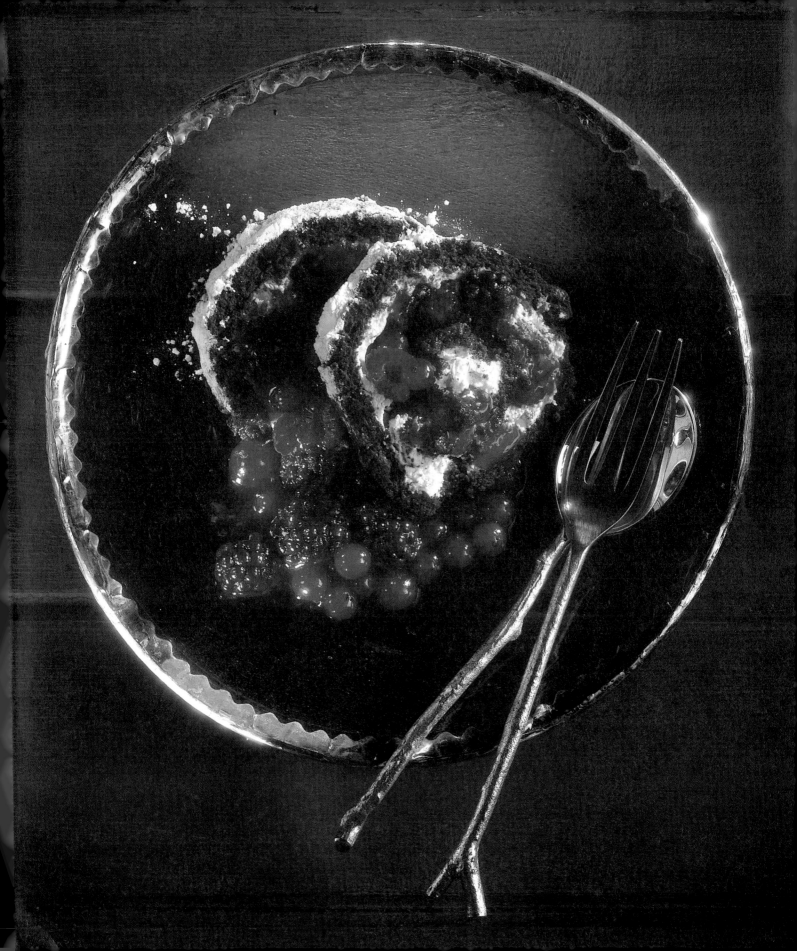